Family - tradit

Other Books By Jay Marshall

The Ten Commandments and Christian Community

The Beatitudes of Christmas

Family Faults:

Healing the Hurts that Threaten the Home

Jay W. Marshall

Almond Rod Enterprises
New Castle, Indiana

Library of Congress Cataloging-in-Publication Data
Marshall, Jay W. (Jay Wade), 1959-
Family Faults: Healing the Hurts that Threaten the Home / Jay W. Marshall
p. cm.
ISBN 0-932970-89-3
1. Family 2. Old Testament 3.Biblical Interpretation I. Title
97-94378
CIP

Library of Congress Catalog Number: 97-94378
International Standard Book Number: 0-932970-89-3
Cover Design by Judi Marshall

To my sisters Kelly, Dee, and Jeanne.
Thank God we survived each other!
May love continue to strengthen those whom
genes initially joined.

CONTENTS

Family Faults

PREFACE

Families have been part of God's design for humanity since the Beginning. The hymnic description of creation in the opening chapter of Genesis speaks of humankind being made as a pair, male and female.[1] Life in the Garden of Eden had barely begun when God decided the human being needed a partner, and created Eve as a suitable helpmate for Adam.[2] Even in that paradise setting, questions, uncertainties, and temptations brought stress, strife, and sin into their relationship. As a result, life together became hard work. Children came along quickly. Like most siblings, Cain's and Abel's competition shoved brotherly love into the background, creating burning hostilities, conflict, and an eventual murder.

So it has been in families ever since. Family relationships and dynamics are a mixture of love and hate, blessing and curse, strength and weakness. Despite those turbulent beginnings described in Genesis, and even with contemporary causes for concern, there is still reason to hope. God originally chose to work through the family unit, and continues to do so. Part of the covenant with Abraham was the creation of a family, which in turn would become a nation and be a blessing to others outside the family.[3] Several Old Testament laws, such as the levirate and harvest laws, helped preserve the family or protect those such as widows and orphans who had no family.[4]

In the New Testament, little is said directly about the family. On occasions, Jesus indicated faith in God may complicate or sever family ties.[5] But when he did speak directly to family issues, Jesus endorsed marriage and mutual love.[6] Likewise, Paul set lofty ideals regarding love between spouses[7] and parental discipline.[8]

These New Testament standards are often heralded as a Scriptural model for the family, which they are. Alone, however, they do little to illuminate the struggles families often endure in the home, and hardly provide a constructive answer for addressing recurring family strife. These limited verses offer good theology, but little practical guidance. Thus, many people, including committed Christians, discover their homes can simultaneously be a secure nest and a fierce battleground. They learn that while the ties of kinship are nearly unbreakable, they are also very fragile. Frederick Buechner was correct when he wrote, "It is within the fragile yet formidable walls of your own family that you learn, or do not learn, what the phrase Human Family means."[9]

The following observations substantiate the situation described above. Since the 1960's, some analysts have wondered if the family unit would or should survive. Numerous studies outline the social and cultural shifts that have affected the family, such as technology, urbanization, the changing roles of women, and expectations within marriage. The bonds of matrimony are more easily broken in this age than ever before. Statistics commonly report that nearly one half of all marriages now end in divorce.[10] The number of children born to unwed, teenage mothers has increased dramatically, affecting three generations in the process: the newborn; the child-mother; and the grandparents, who often assume a large burden of rearing their child's child. The traditional nuclear family consisting of two parents, only one of whom works outside the home, and at least two children now account for only 10% of all families.[11] Family violence has so escalated that, before his retirement, U.S. Surgeon General C. Everett Koop claimed it had reached epidemic proportions. Reported cases of violence between spouses are indeed cause for alarm, as is the claim that three children die each day as a result of abuse or neglect.[12]

A variety of factors can be identified which contribute to the volatile nature of family living. But at a most basic level, there is nothing new about our contemporary situation. When compared to the ideals of Scripture, statistics like these demand our attention. The Christian faith should reinforce hopeful family living and contribute to its healing. This is the goal of this book.

This book is entitled "Family Faults." Though we often use the word "fault" to describe personal imperfections or blame, this book is not about blaming families. The word "fault" is also used to describe a fracture in the earth's crust along which movements and shifts occur, creating earthquakes. As many people worldwide can attest, earthquakes cause major disturbances and disruptions in life. That is the sense in which the word "fault" is being used in this book. In the following pages we will consider those places, qualities or issues which are often the location and cause of earthshaking controversies within the family.

This book is founded upon the belief that God has more to say to families through Scripture than what we often realize. The Old Testament stories involving families contain examples of positive and negative family dynamics. The following chapters will examine several of those stories, with three goals in mind. First, studying them can help define and describe healthy families. Second, paying attention to these stories may help illuminate what is happening in our families and enable us to name the problem(s) that need addressing. Third, the chapters offer suggestions for addressing these dilemmas by highlighting divine answers that are subtly woven throughout the stories. The goal of this study is not faultfinding or casting blame, but discovering ways to avoid the danger zones, as well as pathways to grace and the healing of fractures which already exist.

Chapter 1

ATTENTION K-MART SHOPPERS
GENESIS 3:1-13

Adam & Eve

Have you ever been certain you were in the right place, but were lost nonetheless? I have, though it was more than thirty years ago. When I was a little boy, going shopping with my mother was always a treat. Sometimes it was just a quick trip to little stores in the small town of Siler City. On more exciting trips, we would go to bigger cities like Greensboro or Burlington where there were large department stores, complete with multiple floors and elevators. Even though I loved to go, I would usually get impatient waiting for my mother. In no time at all, it was necessary to look for something to occupy my time.

Do you know a child can actually hide between the clothes hanging on the racks in these stores? With a little wiggling and squirming youngsters can work themselves so far back into the apparel jungle that the garments will close in around their little bodies. If these are long items that hang completely to the floor and cover the feet, even the most trained salesperson has a hard time sniffing out the hidden child. On a good day I could hide for what seemed like an eternity before being found.

However, hiding was not the real reason I enjoyed these trips. I loved to go on these shopping sprees because those stores almost always had a toy department. So while my mother was working through her shopping list, I would drool around those tempting displays, experiment with a few new playthings, and compose a wish list of my very own.

One day we were in a K-Mart store when a similar scenario developed. My mother shopped. I got bored. She gave me permission to go to the toy section, so off I went. I always tried to be careful and observant when venturing out on my own. The story of Hansel and Gretel was quite familiar to me, and I wanted to make sure it was possible to find my way back to where I started. So I would note the section where my mother was shopping, and the number of aisles away from the nearest wall. I would memorize how far I was supposed to go before turning left or right. Once I was securely planted in the toy department, my mother could shop all day if she wanted. I would occasionally retrace my path to see if she were finished, or perhaps to make sure she had not taken advantage of a convenient opportunity to "lose" me! Then I would return to my browsing, daydreaming, and occasional sampling!

To my alarm, on this day when I retraced my steps, my mother was not where I left her. That was a startling experience. So I walked to the end of the empty aisle and looked both ways. There was no sign of her familiar face. I searched the aisles immediately to my right and to my left. She was not to be seen. Panic began to dance in my stomach as I realized I was lost.

To this small kid, being lost in a big K-Mart store was upsetting enough. To make matters worse, this was not Siler City. I could not walk outside and expect someone to recognize me. This was Greensboro, a big city teeming with strange faces and unfamiliar streets. It was a good hour from home by car and probably further than I could walk the rest of my life. Lost, scared, and not knowing where else to look, I began to cry.

I heard of one little fellow who was in a similar situation. As he stood there crying, people felt so helpless and sympathetic they started giving him money. In a few minutes he had collected a couple of dollars. When a woman finally offered to take him to the service desk where they would page his mother, the kid insisted she go away and leave him alone. He did not want to be found just yet because staying lost was more profitable!

No one gave me money. But after a couple of eternal minutes, a kind man approached and asked if I were lost. He then took me to the service desk, and informed the clerk of my predicament. The next thing I heard was a blaring voice over a static-filled intercom: "Attention K-Mart shoppers. Would the mother of Jay Marshall come to the service desk please? We have a lost little boy here." The reason my mother was not where I had left her was not because she had abandoned me. She had finished shopping and had gone looking for me.

That story remains with me as a memorable experience of what it is like to know you are in the right area, and to know the one you are seeking is there, but to be unable to find that person and to be reunited with them. That experience is analogous to what it can be like for individuals, and also for families in their relationships with God.

We know we are in God's world. We believe God is in it. Even though we have been taught that those who seek with all their heart will find God,[13] locating or staying with God in any real, meaningful way sometimes seems beyond our abilities. The truth is that God is searching for us even as we look.[14] But sometimes, for all that effort, we never connect. Maybe we need that K-Mart employee's help: "Attention all creation. Would the Lord please come to the service desk? We have a lost family looking for you."

All the family faults we will consider in the following chapters are rooted in this one: many families are out of touch with God. Some choose not to participate in the life of a local congregation, seeing no need to allocate their time and priorities in this manner. Of those who do participate, several are uncomfortable talking about religion or faith in any significant sense because they are products of an era in which an overly private faith is in vogue. Consequently, the role of faith as part of family life is frequently nonexistent among families who do have a church affiliation. The good news is that families who are lost do not have to stay that way.

There is no better passage of Scripture to illustrate the effects of this fault than the well-known story of Adam and Eve. Lots of explanations, justifications, and interpretations have been posed regarding the First Sin. Christians often only use this story to explain the origin of sin and blame it on someone else. Namely, sin is the fault of the first couple or of the crafty serpent. It seldom occurs to us that perhaps we should understand the story as a description of *our* lives as well as a story about Adam and Eve.

The motivation and definition of the first couple's expulsion are debatable. Free will is a reason commonly offered, insisting human choice was necessary in order for us truly to love God rather than to exist as puppets on a string. Satan's trickery is another often heard motive. A search for wisdom, an inevitable existential development of sorts, is another frequent explanation. While Christians of different persuasions may pose various motives, the results of the garden event are not as diffuse, especially regarding the negative effects on the family unit.

Prior to the apple incident, the story pictures Adam and Eve living in harmony with each other. The Hebrew language describes Eve as a "help mate opposite"Adam. These companions lived in a garden complete with everything they needed for life and happiness. Best of all, they were created with a positive, communion-filled relationship with God. Moreover, they were without shame. THIS was EDEN. Not only was it God's garden; it was a family paradise.

After the incident, a curse and a sense of separation strained the positive communion with God. As a result, where no shame once existed, the family learned about shame experienced because of their nakedness. They were introduced to a new emotion, as fear filled the human heart. It is manifest in the enmity described between humans and snakes, which really depicts distrust of certain things different from us.

Personal pain darkened the scenario as well, represented in the processes of childbirth and toiling in the fields. In place of the "help mate opposite," subordinate relationships entered the cursed family. Because eking out a living was not easy, post-apple Eden included a preoccupation with work complete with the sweat of the brow and the possibility of failure. Paradise, in terms of the garden *and* the family, was history.

The good news is that God did not just give up on this family once they were expelled from the garden. For as Adam and Eve prepared to leave Eden, their Creator clothed them. Later, God protected Cain from revenge, despite his murdering Abel. Both events are evidence that God did not give up on this family. Nevertheless, as a result of their wandering off into the toy section of the garden and losing sight of their heavenly parent, all these difficulties entered their family. Then notice what happened! This couple, whose relationship was now filled with shame, fear, pain, subordination, and a preoccupation with work, decided to become parents! With those issues operating in their family, is it any wonder that Cain killed his brother? Perhaps he was just acting out the problems of the family!

Though we do not talk about it, and perhaps even prefer to deny it, this sort of thing fills every family to some degree. Try as we may, we cannot be completely free of the effect of sin in our lives and in our homes.

For instance, some individuals adopt a shame-based existence and never outgrow it. Our world is filled with individuals who can barely look at themselves in the mirror. Over the course of their lives they have been conditioned to think less of themselves than they really are, or have been stripped of their self-esteem. Perhaps they are ashamed of the way they look because it does not fit glamorous stereotypes. Or they have come to believe that even their best efforts are pitiful, and hope is not an option for them. Often individuals conform to the expectations of others only because they fear the loss of someone else's approval. The exterior endorsement they cherish seems to be the only thing keeping the shame at bay. No doubt, many of these behaviors were learned early in the life of the family, where insufficient amounts of love, affection and affirmation were offered. Now, it is nearly beyond the realm of a possibility to believe they are worthy of their family's love, not to mention the love of God.

Shame is not the only pertinent example. For some individuals, the greatest challenge is living with a distrust of everyone and of anything. Perhaps they are even afraid of their own shadows. Sadly, this characteristic is becoming common in our world. More and more homes are equipped with double deadbolt locks, motion lights, electronic home security systems, and fences around lawns and property. Even in the relatively calm little city where I live, the increases in security features, along with quiet murmurs of alleged threats to safety, are startling. Most of us know someone who can remember a time in the golden age of the past when people did not lock their house doors at night, or were not afraid to walk in dimly lighted parking lots. Few such people remain. Con artists, random shootings, and other intrusive and deceitful actions create an aura of suspicion and distrust.

Certainly, we live in an era when some caution is in order. But it is still sad that such is the case. The effect this has on our mental and spiritual state of mind is particularly distressful. In a land where one is supposedly innocent until proven guilty, many of us relate to strangers from the opposite starting point. We may stop short of calling another guilty, but that person will likely have to earn our trust.

In addition to the shackles of shame and distrust, some suffer with personal pain, be it physical, emotional or spiritual. In my profession as a pastor, I spend a great deal of time listening to people. There is no shortage of heart-wrenching stories of personal crises and family trials. What amazes me is the occasional discovery of medical conditions, of buried, yet tender, family tragedies, or of personal heartaches that seldom are voiced. They may be barely beneath the surface of our emotional stability. Or, they may be calloused with years of bitterness and misery. In either case, if we suffer in silence, the pain demands our attention, drains our energy, and affects our family relationships.

For instance, subordinate relationships permeate most families. Between parents and children this is often necessary and healthy. Between spouses, siblings or in-laws, however, these are not always constructive, and are often brutal.

For some who are workaholics, there is just not enough time in the day for us to do all we need to do (for the good of the family, of course). It is possible that a person works long hours because of love for the job. More often, extreme work schedules are a way of dealing with, or hiding from, personal or family pain.

These are the types of things that enter the family when we are separated from God. They will lead us all around the store as we earnestly try to find a solution for our wounds. What we must learn is that the way we address our deepest needs and improve the family health is by returning to the Heavenly Parent from whom we have been separated.

If God is the source of love, wisdom, and life,[15] we cannot live, teach or champion those qualities as they should be promoted in our families until we are connected with God. Families cannot teach what they have not received any more than a dry river bed can water the countryside. If family members have not received love, they cannot teach love. If they have no faith, they cannot encourage faith in others. If they do not know God through a personal connection, they cannot help such a connection to be made. If only we could hear a voice saying, "Attention K-Mart shoppers. We would like to call your attention to a blue light special. For the next half hour God will be located in the household section."

Admittedly, having a family centered on God is not as easy as it sounds. One night as a bedtime story, there was a father who decided to share with his children how he came into the faith. He tried to tell the story in a way that his four-year-old daughter and two-year-old son could understand. He himself was moved by the experience, and the children listened intently. When he finished the story, he said, "and that is how Daddy got to know that Jesus loves him." After a brief moment of silence, his four-year-old daughter said, "Daddy, next time I want a bedtime story from a book."[16]

I still have a vivid image of my mother gathering the children together one afternoon. We were on an antique bed that once belonged to my great-grandmother. My mother had summoned us for the specific purpose of having a family devotion time. We kids whined. My goodness! You would have thought she sentenced us to hard labor. We complained so much bad she eventually gave in to our requests, but only after getting us to agree to spend some daily time reading the Bible. Even with good intentions, it is difficult for parents to keep a family centered on God.

Formal teaching in the home is a good thing, but it is not the most important thing. As the saying goes, "don't talk the talk if you don't walk the walk." It is more important that leaders in the family walk the walk and live the life, prior to talking the talk. Becoming a family "with God" rather than "without God" has to begin with individuals, especially adults and parents, having their own connection or relationship with God--one that is real, living, and dynamic rather than static, stale, or dead. Only then can we begin to create homes where God's presence is acknowledged and appreciated.

Of course, that takes time. Over a decade ago, a cross cultural study showed that U.S. parents spent less time with their children than parents in almost any other country in the world. For instance, some Russian fathers have said they would never let a day go by without spending two hours with their children. A study conducted in a small U.S. community showed that the average time fathers there spend with their young sons was about thirty-seven seconds per day.[16] One can hope the situation has improved since then, but there are no certain signs this has occurred.

Faith moves from an individual to a family level when the relationships we have with spouse, child, and parents are founded upon and lived out of a personal faith in God. For many of us, that means we have to redefine what it means to be a Christian family. Some families mistake spirituality for an end result. We make it a static thing, teaching a form without form without substance. Family faith for them approaches Paul's words on another subject where he spoke of having a form of godliness but denying the power thereof.[18]

For families to be centered in God, there needs to be more than a shared passive belief in a higher power, or that God is real and "out there," though each of those can be true statements. Being a family connected with God does not mean the family is in church, though families should be participating in the local congregation of their choice. Being connected with God does not mean "the wife is subject to the husband" without recognizing that the husband is also accountable to the wife. It does not mean that "children obey their parents" without realizing that children are gifts from God, and are to be loved rather than provoked, ignored, or abused by their families. Being a family connected with God means that the individual relationships with God contribute to an atmosphere of love, an emphasis on emotional bonding, and a river of communication that includes loving, sharing, encouraging, and when needed, disciplining.

A story told by Grady Nutt provides a snapshot of one way families relate when they are snugly connected with God. Their family had invited the preacher and his wife over for dinner. They had wanted it to be a perfect affair and had drilled the children on proper behavior. Finally, the day came. The meal was cooked. The table was set with a white lace table cloth, the good china, candles, everything. After they sat down, the father had the blessing. When the blessing was over, their nine-year-old daughter reached for her glass of ice-tea and knocked it over. The little brother jumped out of the way, and knocked his over, too. As you can imagine, there was an awkward moment of silence, and a huge tea stain in the middle of this table cloth. But before anyone could say anything, the father knocked his glass over and started to laugh. Then the preacher and his wife knocked theirs over and started to laugh. Finally, even the mother who had worked so hard to create the beautiful table picked up her glass and dumped it on the table as well. As everybody around the table roared with laughter, the father looked down at his daughter right beside him, and he winked at her. As she returned the wink, a tear leaked out and rolled down her cheek. She looked up almost worshipfully at a father who loved her enough to be sensitive to save her from one of life's most embarrassing moments. There were many other responses he could have made in that emotionally-charged situation. The response he chose is a nice example of care within a connected family.

What is your family life like when you are home alone, living together on a day-to-day basis? Think about how being a child of God, a Christian who has reconnected with a searching Heavenly Parent, transforms and shapes the environment of your home. In almost every incident and in every interaction, family members have the opportunity to live the faith and relate in ways that demonstrate God's love for and God's Presence in the family. As the story of Adam and Eve illustrates, one of the most self-destructive tendencies we have is trying to live like a family without the benefit of God's help. A family's life together may not be an Eden-like paradise, but God still cares about your well being and your future. Attention, readers: God is available to help you create a real home.

FOR DISCUSSION

1. Would you describe your life as separated from, or connected with, God? Why do you answer as you do?

2. What does being a Christian family entail for you? Is it a dynamic part of your corporate experience?

3. What practices or traditions currently remind all family members that God is like a loving, searching parent?

4. Are there specific areas where your "walk" doesn't match your "talk?"

5. As a whole, is your family guided and sustained by its relationship with God? What can be done to improve this relationship?

Chapter 2

HOSTILITIES OF THE HEART
GENESIS 25:19-34

It has been said that families are like opinions. Everybody has one, but they aren't all worth repeating. Even if our family is one we would not readily share, it is difficult to overestimate the importance of our families because they form the soil in which the seeds of our lives are initially planted. Their ability or failure to nourish us plays a major role in our development. Since it is a reciprocal process, who we are, in turn, also affects our family's continued growth and development.

I have four siblings. Next to parents, siblings are probably more influential than anyone in our lives during the early years. I have three sisters, all younger than I, and a younger brother who died of SIDS. Some days, thoughts of them warm my heart like a sidewalk in the morning sun. Other days I'm just astounded that we survived at all!

Once, when I was a youngster, I was playing with the handle on the push lawnmower. I repeatedly raised it up and down, just for the sheer thrill of it. On one of those downstrokes my sister, Kelly, who was about two years old at the time, stuck one of her fingers in the right spot to have the very tip snipped off. I thought I had ruined her for good! It may have taken me longer to recover than it did her.

The day my sister, Dee, had her fingers mashed and stuck in a pea sheller was no picnic either. This episode was not my fault! Still, for awhile it seemed I was more upset than she was, though I am sure she bore the majority of the pain! Our family could fill a few large volumes with pulse-raising events like these, but fortunately all the incidents were minor, or at least not fatal.

Siblings everywhere seem to have an innate sense that part of their duty in life is to rename their brothers and sisters, as though the given names registered on the birth certificate are inadequate. If your family is like mine, most of those nick names were a bit embarrassing. I still remember the day my youngest sister Jeanne, whom I had nicknamed Dink, retaliated against some now long forgotten act and called me "Pinky." With all the words in the English language from which to choose, to this day, I have no clue as to why she chose the name Pinky. Fortunately the name was short-lived. Even so, I still cringe a bit every time my family remembers the incident. If you ever had one of those nicknames, you know that if we could only discover where they originated, we would gladly buy them a one-way ticket and send them back.

It has been said that sibling relationships provide our "first social laboratory where we learn how to be a peer. Even when the fights make us cry, we are growing a thick skin, which we need later on as adults; we learn that life doesn't always seem fair; we learn how to forgive."[19] The truth of that statement is obvious if you have brothers and sisters. Siblings survive those times and mature into adulthood. But sometimes, even if we think we have forgiven those hurts, they hang around, lurking in unseen places. Occasionally, they return to haunt us, especially when families gather.

Three sisters were traveling together after a funeral. As they sped along, they shared some fond memories. They sang together in three part harmony, something they had not done in years. They tried to find some common ground in areas of disagreement on issues of women's rights and abortion. The conversation grew tense at times.

Finally the middle sister, who was the family reconciler said, "We're not enemies. Enemies can't sing three part harmony."

And the older sister added, "Or play on the same baseball team," referring to one of their favorite childhood pastimes.

It was then that the youngest sister said irritably, "I never played on your team. Don't you remember? You two and the neighbor boys wouldn't let me play. You said I wasn't old enough or good enough to hit or throw the ball. You made me sit in the announcer's stand and call the games."

The other two sisters were aghast. They did not remember excluding her from their play. The conversation ended with the youngest sister shrugging and saying, "It's all right. I know I'm the lost child."[20]

The blunt truth of the matter is that even though siblings grow up in the same *family*, they never grow up in the *same* family. The emotional, economic, and even physical circumstances of the family are distinct for each child. The first may well be the center of attention, at least until the second one is born. In contrast, the second child never knows what it is like to be the sole recipient of parental affection. Children born early in a marriage when a couple is struggling to make ends meet may not, because of economic necessity, be showered with the same luxuries that might be possible later in life when career advancements have increased a family's earning power. Every parent I have ever heard speak about their children communicates in one way or another the amazing dissimilarities, and thus the different needs, between siblings despite a common gene pool. It is not unusual, and certainly not improper, that good parents respond to their children differently when those responses are based on the individual needs and the family's current situation.

The rest of the story is that even though siblings never grow up in the *same* family, they do grow up in the same *family*. Like a book we have read so often that we know the intricacies of the plot, or a team we have played against on so many occasions we know every play, every strength, every weakness, we know our families better than perhaps we even realize. Consequently, years later, brothers, sisters, parents, families in general, are able to push buttons we have forgotten we even had. They never forget old humiliations and painful nicknames. Sometimes they never let us grow up, which means every family gathering is held on something like the San Andreas fault. It may be calm--or not!

The story of Jacob and Esau speaks to this type of family fault. As we trace the conflict through the stories of their lives, we are given a window through which to observe the effects their hostilities have on everyone involved in the web of intimate relationships.

The trouble began even before the twins were born, as they tossed and turned prior to birth. Competitiveness was an inherent part of this relationship. Jacob was grasping at Esau, reaching for priority and prominence, even as the two exited the womb. As is always the case, each child had his own characteristics, his own preferences, his own skills. As often happens, some of those individual qualities promoted parental preferences which can lead to the adoption of family favorites. Isaac preferred Esau; Rachel favored Jacob.

With that background, stew was not the only thing simmering the day Esau returned hungry from the hunt. It seems Jacob had always wanted what Esau had. He coveted the preference of his father. He wished to be the recipient of the birthright. He wanted the blessing to which only the firstborn male was entitled in that society. In that culture, and to some extent in our own, these were endorsements of one's power and prestige. They enhanced one's authority and wealth. On that fateful day when Esau met Jacob, Esau's hunger overpowered his brain. So while he could think of nothing but food, Jacob negotiated the deal of a lifetime. His older brother forfeited his birthright for a single bowl of stew. Esau left with his stomach filled, but despising his birthright. Hostility was born in Esau's heart that day. A fault was created that could cause damage of earthquake proportions.

That incident was only the beginning. Later, with the help of his mother (because he was her favorite), Jacob tricked his father, Isaac, and stole the blessing of the firstborn. This occurred during a deathbed ritual which transferred the power, wealth and authority of the patriarch to the firstborn son. As a result of this second act of thievery, in Genesis 27:41 we discover Esau plotting his revenge, vowing to kill his brother.

On a historical level, one may speak of this story as a conflict between individuals, or even an indication of ongoing friction between certain tribal groups who traced their lineage to these two brothers. From a literary perspective, we may also focus on the plot development and the family dynamics within the story, and at that point find meaning with more contemporary relevance. This story illustrates that family favorites led to family secrets--secret hurts and secret plots. In turn these secrets, combined with fears, insecurities, and the competitiveness of certain family members, created volatile and explosive possibilities. The resultant mix created the kind of instability that can give birth to new family members, namely hostilities of the heart. These hostilities forced this family, and they force us, to live on the fault line which rumbles every time a new hostility is born or an old one is disturbed. The rest of Jacob's and Esau's lives were lived sifting through the debris caused by the disturbance of this fault.

The truth of the matter is that the issue is not really about Jacob's dislike of Esau. It is about maturation and confidence. It is about Jacob's struggling to discover his identity and to become convinced of his own merits. This becomes clear when we pay attention to his dreams. The evening that Jacob fled from Esau's wrath, he dreamed of a ladder to heaven. The ladder symbolizes a connection with the divine in which God says "I am your God and I will bless you."[21] Although there was cumulative evidence over the years which suggested God was indeed blessing him,[22] Jacob apparently was not convinced. Many years later, on the night before Jacob's first meeting with his brother since the theft of Esau's blessing, Jacob wrestled with God and with himself over his identity. Again, the issue was God's blessing.

This story is loaded with insights regarding family conflicts and their resolution. Jacob and Esau were simply a pair of brothers trying to become the individuals they were created to be. When they were doing that, and when we are doing that, on the most basic level, we are trying to discover the presence and call of God in our lives. The two brothers were hindered in that process because no one in their family was helping them in this task. Perhaps they were too busy trying to find it themselves.

Their scenario reminds me of the truth expressed in a story of a young boy called upon by his teacher to stand before his classmates and tell them what he wanted to be when he grew up. As he stood shuffling and twisting before the audience of his peers, he said firmly, "When I grow up, I want to be possible."

His teacher had heard her share of strange goals during her career, but this was a first! She asked, "Possible? What do you mean, you want to be possible?"

Her student replied, "My parents are always saying, 'Billy, you're impossible.' So, when I grow up, I just want to be possible."

We have no record of Jacob or Esau receiving this type of negative reinforcement, but it is an apt description of their dilemma. They were constantly disturbed by quakes of the heart and rifts in the family. This is, in fact, a common scenario in families. Hurts and hostilities accumulate, eventually reshaping our identities, not to mention disguising the family landscape.

Jack Canfield tells a story of visiting several Buddhist temples while in Bangkok. One of those was the Temple of the Golden Buddha. Though it is small, about thirty feet by thirty feet, it contains a ten and a half foot tall, solid gold Buddha. It weighs more than two and one half tons and is valued at $196,000,000.

Back in 1957, a group of monks from a monastery had to relocate a clay Buddha from their temple to a new location. When the crane began to lift the giant idol, the weight of it was so tremendous that it began to crack. What's more, rain began to fall. The head monk, who was concerned about damage to the sacred Buddha, decided to lower the statue back to the ground and cover it with a large canvas tarp to protect it from the rain.

Later that evening, the head monk went to check on the statue. He shined his flashlight under the tarp to see if it was staying dry. As the light reached the crack, he noticed a little gleam shining back and thought it strange. As he took a closer look at this gleam of light, he wondered if there might be something underneath the clay. He fetched a chisel and hammer from the monastery and began to chip away. As he knocked off shards of clay, the little gleam grew brighter and bigger. After many hours of labor, the monk stood face to face with an extraordinary solid gold Buddha.

Historians believe that several hundred years before the head monk's discovery, the Burmese army was about to invade Thailand. The monks covered their precious golden Buddha with a covering of clay to keep their treasure from being looted by the Burmese. Unfortunately, it appears that the Burmese slaughtered all the monks and the secret of the golden Buddha remained intact until that day in 1957.

As Canfield flew home from Bangkok, he was struck by the insight that, "We are all like the clay Buddha covered with a shell of hardness created out of fear, and yet underneath each of us is something like that golden statue--we might say a golden Christ, or a golden essence which is our real self. Somewhere along the way between the ages of two and nine, we begin to cover up our golden essence, our natural self. Much like the monk with the hammer and the chisel, our task now is to discover our true essence once again."[23]

That is another way of describing Jacob's conflict with Esau. In spite of the conflict and through the pain, Jacob discovered the essence of his identity. He learned to accept the reality that God was blessing him as he was and for who he would be as a person of the covenant. His story is like a silhouette whose shadowy movements remind us of our own struggles. That is no surprise, because our Christian journey of faith is also about discovering those very things.

It is worth our notice that family reconciliation did not occur until Jacob discovered his essence. He remained hidden behind his own false outer shell until God's penetrating light pierced its cracks, and Jacob's identity was so shaped by his relationship with his Creator that he called himself by a different name. Only the blessing of God can soothe the hostilities of the heart.

I have had the privilege of sharing in major and minor rites of passage with families in over fourteen years of ministry now. As a participant and an observer, I can say that our families, which should be the safest place for us, filled with the most affirming relationships in the world, often fail us in some crucial ways. Secrets, favorites, and fears give birth to resentments and hostilities. In response, like Jacob, we steal and run. Like a boxer, we jab and weave. Like the monks and their golden statue, we slowly hide ourselves behind a protective covering until we hardly resemble our true selves. Then we spend hours wondering why our life and our family are such a mess. This is not a healthy way to live. The Scripture story teaches us that the one way to overcome those family hostilities toward what others have, what they are, and how they make us feel, is to address those issues based on who we are as children of God, blessed by God.

You have been chosen by your Creator to be a part of this incredible universe. To you has been given the gift of life. God walks with you through life's challenges, even wrestling with you so that you capture the meaning of your existence. This relationship is filled with Divine Blessing, and needs only to be discovered by you. With that blessing intact, the strife that fuels many family conflicts will disintegrate. Only when one's relationship with God begins to transform our identities can the competitive fractures in our families truly be healed. That is true for any family we have, whether biological, faith, or otherwise. Until they are resolved, the fault fraught with hostilities of the heart can deny us family unity and a cohesive community.

It is my prayer that you will discover who you are as a child of God. Secure in that identity, like Jacob, return home. Share the blessing and help heal the family fault created by hostilities of the heart.

FOR DISCUSSION

1. What nicknames did your family give you? Did you like them?

2. Do Jacob and Esau's sibling rivalry resemble any rivalries in your own household?

3. What are the greatest sources of hostility in your home between siblings, parents or other family members? What triggers their resurfacing?

4. What sort of help do you expect from God in resolving these conflicts?

5. What can you personally do to help resolve these conflicts?

Chapter 3

TOSSED TREASURES
II Samuel 15:1-12

Robert Fulghum tells a touching story about taking care of family treasures. One day as he prepared to leave his house for work, his young daughter Molly handed him two bags. One regular lunch sack, and one tattered sack, held together by duct tape, staples and paper clips.

"Why two bags?" he asked.

She said, "The other one is something else."

He persisted, "What's in it?"

She answered, "Just some stuff--take it with you." So he did.

At midday, while hurriedly scarfing down his real lunch, he tore open Molly's bag, and shook out the contents. He discovered two hair ribbons, three small stones, a plastic dinosaur, a pencil stub, a tiny seashell, two animal crackers, a marble, a used lipstick, a small doll, two chocolate kisses, and thirteen pennies. It made him smile. Then, rising to hustle off to all the important business of the afternoon, he swept the desk clean--into the wastebasket--leftover lunch, Molly's junk and all. There wasn't anything in there he needed.

That evening as he relaxed reading the paper, Molly came to stand beside him.

"Where's my bag?" she asked.

Absentmindedly, he responded, "What bag?"

"You know. The one I gave you this morning."

He answered, "I left it at the office. Why?"

She said, "I forgot to put this in it," and she handed over a note.

"Besides, I want it back."

"Why?" her father asked.

Molly explained, "Those are my things in the sack, Daddy, the ones I really like. I thought you might like to play with them, but now I want them back. You didn't lose the bag did you Daddy?" Tears puddled in her eyes.

He answered with a lie, "Oh no, I just forgot to bring it home."

Reassured, Molly said, "Bring it tomorrow, okay?"

As she hugged his neck with relief, he unfolded the note that had not been put into the sack. It read "I love you, Daddy."

As he looked at his little girl's face, he realized she was right. What was in that sack was "something else." She had given him her treasures. All that a seven-year-old held dear. Love in a paper sack. And he had missed it. Not only missed it, but had thrown it in the wastebasket because "there wasn't anything there he needed."

It was a long trip back to the office that night, but there was nothing else to be done. He was sorting it all out when the janitor came in to do his chores.

The janitor asked, "Lose something?"

Fulghum answered, "Yeah, my mind."

The janitor replied, "What's it look like and I'll help you find it."

After washing the mustard off the dinosaurs and spraying the whole thing with breath-freshener to kill the smell of onions, he carefully smoothed out the wadded ball of brown paper into a semi-functional bag and put the treasures inside and carried the whole thing home gingerly, like an injured kitten. The next evening he returned it to Molly, who asked no questions.

After dinner, he asked her to tell him about the stuff in the sack. So she took it all out, a piece at a time and placed the objects in a row on the dining room table. It took a long time to tell. Everything had a story, a memory, or was attached to dreams and imaginary friends. These were her treasures, entrusted to his care. How could he have so foolishly tossed them aside?[24]

Fulghum's experience may be like an echo of something in your own life. His story is one that leads into the area of yet another family fault. Have you ever given someone your treasure, only to have it tossed? Do you remember how it felt to see your valuables cast aside like junk, like worthless clutter, like trash? Have you ever had your life, your love, your trust strewn to the wayside as though they didn't matter?

Have your hopes, your dreams, your fears been wadded up and canned as if there was nothing important there? Have you ever made a commitment to be family, intimately relating to and sticking with these people when no one else will, only to have your offerings, your life, your feelings pushed aside like worthless trinkets?

Or perhaps you have been the tosser, carelessly casting aside the gifts of love that had been entrusted to you. Perhaps you did not realize the value they had. Maybe you were not aware of the harm being done. Or perhaps you did realize but simply did not care once you measured them alongside *your* dreams.

The garbage heap of tossed treasures is located adjacent to the family fault line of disrespect. Such disregard of others is rooted in the sin of self-centeredness. It is often fertilized by a wide range of emotions from apathy to envy. Each of those is rooted in issues within our hearts that connect to our relationship with God, to our contentment with ourselves and to our understanding of the corporate, cooperative nature of families in particular and society in general.

The stories about Absalom's life invite us to see and feel, from a Scriptural perspective, the havoc that a lack of respect can create among family members. Ironically enough, the name "Absalom" means "my father is peace," yet peace is nowhere near the appropriate description for the relationship he had with his father David. Their life together was like a B-movie with too many bad sequels. Each scenario replayed similar themes of volatile strife, scheming deceit, and fragile attempts at reconciliation.

The deck may have been stacked against Absalom from the outset. He was so good looking he could put the latest fashion model to shame. He had not a single blemish from head to toe. His special pride was his hair, which was a gorgeous mane. He only trimmed it when it became too heavy for him. The trimmings alone tipped the scales at three and a half pounds. Good looking. Great hair. On top of it all, he was royalty. He sounds like a person who would be easy to follow and trust.

Absalom was a "take action" type of person. Unfortunately, instead of positive brain-storming or adaptation to not getting his own way, much of his action was revenge-oriented. When his older brother raped his sister, Absalom threw a party, got his brother drunk, and had him killed. That little plot resulted in temporary exile from his father, the king. When the king's army commander, Joab, refused to win Absalom an audience with his father, the impulsive Absalom set Joab's barley fields on fire. That got Joab's attention! Absalom would not be ignored.

Revenge-oriented is not the only appropriate description of this son. The events in the text chosen for this chapter occurred after King David and his son were reconciled. Apparently Absalom was not *too* glad to be back in the king's good graces. Any penitence felt and lessons learned in exile were quickly forgotten. For in this story, this rebellious son sat outside the city gate where people passed by on their way to the court where the king judged their complaints. There, the young prince would lament to the people passing by, "if only *I* were the judge in the land, your case would be heard and I'd see that justice was done." As Absalom continued to woo the people with his feigned compassion, verse six says "he stole the hearts of the people of Israel." This thief of hearts, with his false sympathy and pseudo-concern, was undermining his father's authority! In addition to being motivated by revenge, Absalom's actions reveal he was also an instigator.

As I Samuel 15 unfolds, this good-looking, disrespecting, glory-seeking son of the king even initiated a conspiracy to overthrow his father and assume control of the entire household and kingdom. King David fled for his life, leaving the whole countryside weeping at his departure (v23). That is one effect of disrespect in the family. As it drives individuals away from families, tears are a common sight.

Absalom's actions were filled with disrespect for human life. They had no regard for family authority, or for his father's authority in particular. He cared little for his professional and family reputation. He exhibited no appreciation for the grace that allowed him to return to the family after murdering his brother. Absalom was tossing family treasures aside, scattering disrespect along the way, all in pursuit of his dreams.

When we think about families and what makes them important, or enjoyable, words like "love" usually sit atop the list. The word "respect" should also be a high priority term. It is true that some Scriptures warn against being a "respecter of persons," in the sense of favoritism or undue veneration. That is not what is being called for here. As used here, respect refers to treating others with common decency, and valuing the other as a person of integrity worthy of our respect. Respect of this type is rooted in the goodness of God's creation and in the morality that accompanies the faith relationship with God.

That such respect is lacking in this story is obvious if we pay special attention to what is happening in the narrative. In this family, complete with parental and sibling relationships, we discover a son who desires to mature, develop, and become a person and a force in his own right. He possesses a desire for independence and recognition.

Goodness knows, we want all those things for the people we love. Find your identity. Discover your calling. Get a job. Move out of your parents' house before the age of forty. We all know what it is like to possess those desires because it was a part of our own life processes.

However, Absalom possesses one quality that we should hope and pray is absent in our own lives and families: a complete lack of respect for the lives, the plans, the desires of everyone else to the degree that we trample and toss the family treasures entrusted to us. The lesson we learn from the story is that when respect is lacking in our families, disrespect will rule in its stead.

In minor cases, this disrespect may be like a dog whose bark is worse than its bite. Such was the case with a promising young executive who quit his job, and before leaving, stopped in to say goodbye to his boss. The boss lamented, "I'm sorry to see you go. Actually, you've been like a son to me--sassy, impatient, demanding, and loud!"[25]

However, the troubles which explode from the fault line of disrespect generally do not stop with loud and sassy. They can also easily lead to physical violence, emotional exile, and deceitful efforts to steal someone else's domain. Such was the case with Absalom's family. The story illustrates that living along this fault line is an invitation to disaster.

We should not fail to notice that all of this occurs under the umbrella of God's covenant with David and his family. *This* was the chosen family. In addition to whatever prestige this position carried, it also brought the tremendous responsibility of exemplifying holy, righteous, covenant living to the remainder of the Israelite kingdom. That such tragedy could erupt in the "first family" of Israel adamantly teaches that even as God desires to bless and build the family, it is possible that our own motivations are so out of step with God's leadings that we dilute the effects of the Divine blessing. Nowhere in God's desire for the family is there room for the sort of things created by this family fault.

As we move from story to application, let us ask, "What is it like in our families? Are we respecting each other, or are we tossing treasures left and right as we march toward personal goals and carry out our individual agendas?" Most likely, if treasures are being tossed in your family, it is not as dramatic and shocking as Absalom's exploits. But do not be deceived. Like that old tattered paper bag filled with "something else," love, trust, hopes, and dreams come in all shapes and sizes. They may appear as years of fidelity, or whispered secrets, or vulnerable admissions. They may come to us in the form of seemingly trivial gifts which are in fact spontaneous expressions of deep love and adoration. In whatever form they are manifest, when we fail to recognize them, treasure tossing does occur in families in some common ways.

As an example, consider the story of Larry and JoAnn, who were an ordinary couple. They lived in an ordinary house on an ordinary street. Like any other ordinary couple, they struggled to make ends meet and to do the right things for their children. They were an ordinary couple in yet another way. They had their squabbles. Much of their conversation concerned what was wrong in their marriage and who was to blame. Things deteriorated to the point that, sort of like Absalom, most of their relationships with family were spent getting what they wanted and needed, even at the expense of others. They were tossing quite a few family treasures in the process. "Respect" was just the name of an Aretha Franklin song.

Until one day the most extraordinary event took place. Larry said, "You know JoAnn, I've got a magic chest of drawers. Every time I open them, they're full of socks and underwear. I want to thank you for filling them all these years."

JoAnn stared at him over the top of her glasses. "What do you want?"

This was not the first time Larry had done something odd, so JoAnn pushed the incident out of her mind until a few days later. That was when he said, "Thank you for recording so many correct check numbers in the ledger this month. You put down the right numbers fifteen out of sixteen times. That's a record."

Jo Ann looked up from her mending. "Larry, you're always complaining about me recording the wrong check numbers. Why stop now?"

"No reason. I just wanted you to know I appreciate the effort you're making."

JoAnn just shook her head, went back to her mending, and mumbled, "What's got into him?" Nevertheless, the next day when JoAnn wrote a check at the grocery store, she glanced at her checkbook to confirm that she had put down the right check number. "Why do I suddenly care about those dumb check numbers?" she asked herself. She tried to disregard the incident, but Larry's strange behavior intensified.

One evening he said, "JoAnn, that was a great dinner. I appreciate all your effort. Why, in the past fifteen years I'll bet you've fixed over fourteen thousand meals for me and the kids."

Then, it was "Gee, JoAnn the house looks spiffy. You've really worked hard to get it looking so good."

And even, "Thanks JoAnn for just being you. I really enjoy your company."

JoAnn was growing worried. "Where's the sarcasm, the criticism?"

Whatever was wrong, Larry didn't get over it. Day in and day out he continued focusing on the positive in ways that honored her treasures. As he honored her treasure, the territory around this fault line grew calm. Over the weeks, JoAnn grew more accustomed to her mate's unusual behavior and occasionally even gave him a grudging, "Thank you." Over time, JoAnn's step became a little lighter, her self-confidence higher. She didn't seem to have as many blue moods anymore.

That would be the end of the story, except for the fact that one day another most extraordinary event took place. One day, Jo Ann said, "Larry, I want to thank you for going to work and providing for us all these years. I don't think I've ever told you how much I appreciate it."

Though Jo Ann has often asked, Larry has never revealed the reason for his dramatic change of behavior. It will likely remain one of life's mysteries. But one thing is for certain. Family life has improved in their household since they began honoring each other's treasures with a little respect.[26]

Respect is a contribution we can all make to the health and vitality of our families. It is not expensive to give, but it is priceless when received. It promotes peace, encourages harmony, and inspires reconciliation.

As God continues to bless us and works to build up our families, may we each learn to be mindful of the treasures with which we have been entrusted. And may our homes and our relationships be filled with respect.

FOR DISCUSSION

1. What is the most precious treasure you have shared with your family in the last year? How was it received?

2. Are there occasions when you felt someone "tossed your treasures?" If that still causes the fault line of disrespect to rumble, can you gently express your thoughts on the matter to your family?

3. Have you tossed someone's treasures recently, inadvertently or otherwise? What can you do to restore their treasure?

4. Is respect easy to come by in your family, for all parties?

5. Name three new actions or affirmations your family will institute to help insure your family avoids the snares illustrated by Absalom.

Chapter 4

CROSSING CUSTOMS
GENESIS 29:14-30

The train clanked and rattled through the suburbs of Tokyo on a drowsy spring afternoon. The car was comparatively empty--a few parents with their kids in tow, some folks going shopping. A man named Terry sat on that train and gazed absently at the passing drab houses and dusty hedgerows.

At one station the doors opened. Suddenly the afternoon quiet was shattered by a man bellowing violent, incomprehensible curses. The man staggered into the train car. He was big, drunk and dirty. Screaming, he swung at a woman holding a baby. The blow sent her spinning into the laps of an elderly couple. It was a miracle that the baby was unharmed.

Everyone jumped up and scrambled toward the other end of the car. The crazed man aimed a kick at the retreating back of an old woman but missed as she scuttled to safety.

This so enraged the drunk that he grabbed the metal pole in the center of the car and tried to wrench it out of its stanchion. The train lurched ahead, the passengers frozen with fear. Terry stood up. He had been putting in a solid eight hours of Aikido training every day for the past three years. The trouble was, his martial arts skill was untested in actual combat. As students of Aikido, they were not allowed to fight.

`His teacher had said again and again, "Aikido is the art of reconciliation. Whoever has the mind to fight has broken his connection with the universe. If you try to dominate people, you're already defeated. We study how to resolve conflict, not how to start it."

Terry listened to those words. He tried hard. But in his heart he wanted an absolutely legitimate opportunity whereby he might save the innocent by destroying the guilty. This situation seemed to be it. He rose to his feet.

Seeing him stand, the drunk recognized a chance to focus his rage. Terry gave him a look of disgust and dismissal. He planned to take this turkey apart, but the drunk had to make the first move. He wanted him mad, so he pursed his lips and blew him an insolent kiss.

With that the drunk hollered, "All right! You're gonna get a lesson!" He gathered himself for a rush at his opponent. In that moment, they stood there face-to-face. Lines drawn. Feeling like enemies. Ready to explode.[27]

Families have moments like that, though hopefully minus the drunken stupor and without excess enthusiasm for martial arts. With or without them, families spend some time on the road of life riding in the same train car, so to speak. There are moments when a relative's conduct, personal goals and ambitions, or approach to life does not set well with other passengers on the family train, and the others decide to take charge of the situation. Those become moments of confrontation where one wrong move could lead to a family explosion.

The story of Jacob and Laban is just such a powder keg situation. These two, plus Rachel and Leah, are tumbling around another family fault area, toying with disaster. They live in that place where conflicts escalate because of different expectations, divergent points of view, or dissimilar standards of evaluation, which in turn are used to control other family members. They are living near the fault caused by family customs.

Put yourself in Jacob's place, momentarily. Imagine going on a journey to find a spouse, as he did. As you stop at a well for water, your eyes behold a vision of loveliness. It is a moment of mesmerization. This is the angel of your dreams. The chemistry sizzles. Excitement swells. It is a magical encounter! By the day's end, you are meeting family and passing all the unwritten, but non-negotiable, tests. A long engagement is agreed upon, which includes your working for your beloved's family in order to gain the right to marry your newly-found love. Imagine seven years of sweat. Three hundred sixty-four weeks of backbreaking, muscle-aching toil. Two thousand, five hundred, forty-eight days of counting down the moments until the grand union occurs.

The day of the wedding finally arrives. It is a storybook moment! The invited guests are generous. The feast is tasty. The veiled bride and anxious groom both show up, which is always a plus! They survive the festivities. The wedding happens without interference, and the couple spends their first night together. After the wedding is consummated, the bride's veil is removed. Instead of the love of your life, imagine as Jacob experienced, this shocking sight: you have married the wrong sister. You have just spent the night declaring your love and promising the moon to Leah, not Rachel.

Admittedly, a scenario such as this is difficult for us to imagine. Our culture still perpetuates the superstition that it is bad luck for a bride and groom to see each other on their wedding day prior to the ceremony. But even if the bride chooses to wear a veil over her face, a practice I seldom see observed, the veil is lifted at some point during the ceremony, likely for the wedding kiss. So the chance of such a surprise in a contemporary wedding is slight.

Apparently, wedding customs in Jacob's culture allowed such a scheme to materialize. According to the story, that is exactly what happened to him. As crafty as Jacob was, one would expect him to be on guard against such shenanigans. It is surprising he did not at least sneak a peek at his bride, but he did not. When Jacob discovered the switch and confronted his father-in-law regarding this deception, Laban offered this excuse: "It is not our custom to marry the younger daughter before the older one."

Custom?? I personally would need a better explanation! This is the type of crucial information I would want ahead of time, as in before beginning seven years of sweaty, hard labor. It would rank right up there with knowing if serial killings, holiday sing-alongs, and prolonged family visits ran in the family.

Jacob had inadvertently married Leah, the other sister. Though Leah did have weak eyes,[28] she was probably a fine woman. But she could never have been good enough, for it was Rachel who made Jacob's heart flutter. He could not be content until she was his wife. To earn the right to marry Rachel, he agreed to work seven more years for Laban. Three hundred sixty-four more weeks. Two thousand, five hundred forty-eight more days. But it was never quite the same. As someone has said, it's seldom a wise idea to be married to two sisters at the same time, even under the best of circumstances!

Pay attention to the dynamics of this story! That Jacob was duped is unquestionable. As support for his deceit, Laban appealed to family customs. However, the truth is that "custom" was a camouflage for something else. This one incident is but the beginning of a pattern.

The next rumbling along this fault involved Laban's short-changing Jacob of his share of the herds. In return for his labor, Jacob was to receive a certain portion of Laban's herds so that he could build the wealth and economic self-sufficiency of his own family household. Laban tried different schemes to prevent Jacob from accumulating wealth of his own. Again, family customs were used as an excuse to manipulate situations. It allowed Laban to extract unfair labor, and to build family wealth for himself at the expense of the younger generation in hopes of keeping them dependent. Laban even admitted that he wanted to keep Jacob around because God blessed his household through the affiliation with Jacob. By Laban's own admission, much of what was disguised as custom was rooted in a desire for power, control, and God's blessing. Family customs were being used to enforce structure and order that were to Laban's advantage but which deprived Jacob, Rachel and Leah of the ability to take definite shape as a family in their own right.

All families have customs, though we usually cannot remember how they began. Nevertheless, they are carved into the stone wall of a family's collective consciousness. For example, a story circulates about a young woman who cooked a ham every Thanksgiving. In preparing this dish, she always cut off about one fourth of the meat and cooked it alongside the remainder of the ham. When this practice was questioned, she responded, "I cut off the back part of the ham because that is the way we have always done it in my family."

This answer proved unsatisfactory, so the woman appealed to a higher court: her mother, from whom she learned the practice. She asked, "Mother, why do we cut off the end of the ham before we cook it?"

Her mother replied, "I do not know why *you* do it. I did it because my pan was too small to hold the entire ham in one piece."

Many family customs persist long after their origins have been forgotten. I have inadvertently violated so many of them since I have been married that if they came with prison sentences, I would probably never again see the light of day.

Customs can include things like holiday traditions. Which holidays are celebrated and which ones are not? Of those which are celebrated, which ones are mandatory and which are optional? Satisfying these expectations grows complicated when children marry or parents remarry. My wife, Judi, and I had to negotiate a list of observed special occasions because her family's list and mine did not match. She wanted more than Christmas, birthdays and anniversaries, while I wanted to avoid celebrating every Hallmark holiday on the calendar. Once the different customs are identified, it is also important to know what punishment, such as silence, family gossip, or shame, is issued for those who dare to violate the custom.

Another area where crossed customs result in a clash is in the realm of family values. A simple, modest lifestyle may be the preferred manner of living. Or, a family may prefer a more flamboyant, extravagant approach. This translates into conflicts such as saving versus spending, style of home, models of an automobile, cost of clothing, and more. The fault becomes even more unstable when the extended family tries to intervene with the goal of promoting their values so that their "little girl or boy" may live in the manner she or he deserves. Many marriages have crumbled due to the tremors of this fault.

Education is another common area where values may differ. College may be essential according to one family's unwritten bylaw. In fact, there may be a grand tradition leading to one particular prestigious institution. In contrast, there are still families where not only is college not deemed necessary, but even a high school diploma appears optional. Anything beyond that twelve-year achievement is considered a waste of good time and money.

Or consider the subject of disciplining children. There has always been a difference of opinion on the subject. Recent years have seen physical means of discipline fall out of public favor, though this is by no means universally accepted. For some families, spankings are out and "time outs" are in. By some standards, yesterday's stern discipline is today's abuse. During a recent premarital counseling session, it became clear that one party preferred to "let kids be kids." The spouse-to-be expected better manners, less rowdy behavior, and was willing to scold and spank to achieve this goal. Without doubt, this is an area where this particular couple will have to endure a few fault tremors before they reconcile their differences on the subject.

Approach to religion is another place where values often differ. There was a time when my own religious group, the Society of Friends, required its members to marry only persons who were Friends, or willing to become Friends. Violating this practice could lead to disownment by the group. I have at least one ancestor who suffered this fate because he married outside the Society. If such practices were still condoned, I would have been disowned as well. On the surface, such a requirement appears to be a controlling, even meddlesome, position. While I do not wish for it to be re-instituted, the reason for the strict discipline is easy to understand. Common religious values insure a greater probability of agreement on the role and type of religious faith lived and taught within that family unit. It is disappointing that this is a low priority item for many couples who intend to marry and begin a family. If the practice of religion is important to only one member of a family, this area will likely become a fault area at some point during their life together.

There are many other areas where it is important to understand family customs as well. They cover a wide range of topics, including the expected roles of husband, wife and children to each other *and* to the extended family. Proper communication channels and methods, such as direct or grapevine communication, are also prime areas for conflict. Violating any one of these customs is nearly enough to bring the house crumbling down around us.

I vividly remember almost causing the earth to stand still and prompting the end of civilization as we know it the evening I participated in the first multi-generational meal with my in-laws. After the blessing, I helped myself to the dish which was sitting directly in front of me. Remembering my best manners which said sharing was important, not only did I limit myself to a small portion, but I passed the bowl to the right. I could have easily passed it to the left, but the person on my left was occupied with another platter while the person on the right was staring at a lonely yeast roll on her plate.

The exact moment contact was made with the party on my right was like walking through those metal detectors at the airport. The etiquette siren was sounded by the middle sister of the in-law family. Where was I raised? Didn't I know anything? Didn't I know that food was always passed clockwise? I asked "why," thinking perhaps some unknown formal rule of etiquette had been breached. Instead, I learned it was not because of formal etiquette. It was because of family custom, decreed by her mother, so that everything was passed in the same direction. Now, whenever I am at their house, I pass food in a clockwise direction. I still do not think it is essential, but there is something to be said for prompt service!

You have probably violated your own share of such taboos. Family customs can be innocent. They are simply the way things are done. They are not necessarily right or wrong, or better or worse. It is just the way they are done. They range from not eating mustard on sandwiches, to not frequenting certain types of establishments. Some carry a little more force and, if we allow it, guilt and shame upon violation.

Judi and I joke that if there had been an 11th commandment it would have said, "Remember the Big Drake Christmas and keep it holy. On that day, neither you, nor your spouse, nor any family member, nor your pets will even think of making plans if it means not attending the Big Drake Christmas." It is a nice event, if you like family reunions. As people grow older, reunions often become more important. But when we lived in North Carolina and could not attend the Indiana-based event, we would get nice letters sharing the events of the day. It usually contained a reminder that fifty-five of fifty-seven family members were present.

If we are not careful, and perhaps even when we are, there comes a point where family customs become law-like. At that point, family custom is not something we do because we enjoy it. It is something we do because it is expected of us, even if we do not like it. Then, the issue becomes touchy. Family customs may lose their innocence. They may be used as power over members to create conformity and uniformity, to keep some people in and others out.

In moments like those, the term "family customs" takes on a new nuance. It becomes more than "the way we do things." Customs are then more like the checkpoint at a nation's border where we must prove who we are, and give acceptable reasons for wanting to cross to the other side. If we enter without approval, we can expect to be harassed and persecuted in subtle and not so subtle ways. Perhaps families would operate more smoothly if we *did* all pass through a customs checkpoint and declare our baggage so there are no secret motives and agendas hidden away. But such is not the case. Consequently, this fault line threatens to rumble.

When this fault line is active, family members--our own flesh and blood--are disregarded, disowned, even written out of wills for things as petty as bowing when they should have curtseyed. Quite often, like Aikido man and the drunk, our differences cause us to stand face-to-face with our familial adversary, wondering what it will take to resolve the conflict once and for all. And, eventually the frustration reaches the point where we are willing to lunge at them if we think there is the tiniest chance we can succeed.

In the case of Jacob's family, who in the story has been chosen by God to carry on the covenant blessing, they struggled for years to live peacefully and prosper. They tried to congeal as a family while abiding by Laban's rules. But it was a no-win situation. Even when they outsmarted him, they had stooped to his level. So they decided to move away. Truthfully, if a resolution cannot be worked out, disengaging from the situation is sometimes the only way to heal this fault.

Of course, moving comes with its own set of pains. It is interesting that before Jacob's family departed, Rachel swiped her father's teraphim. These were religious figurines thought to help insure God's blessing. Her theft of the teraphim, and Laban's comment about keeping Jacob around so that God will bless him, says something about the nature of these custom conflicts. Many times they are merely devices to ensure our personal power and prosperity. Though we should not do so, deep within our hearts and minds many of us still interpret power and prestige as signs of God's blessing. This in itself suggests that the need to enforce customs and to connect our ordered worlds with God's will is related to our need to feel connected with and blessed by God. That is a good need, but there must be a better way to achieve and receive it. There is a better way than Laban's controlling agenda. There are more useful choices than relocating, as did Jacob, Rachel and Leah.

By the way, in the conflict between the Aikido student and the drunken man, a fraction of a second before he could move, someone shouted, "Hey!" They both turned to see a little old Japanese man. He was seventyish, looking immaculate as he sat there in his kimono. He beamed delightedly at the drunk, as though he had a most important, most welcome secret to share. The old man said, "C'mere and talk with me."

The big man roared, "Why should I talk to you?"

Terry remained prepared to strike, but it was not necessary. In amazement, he watched as the old man developed a conversation--created one out of thin air. In a short time, they were talking about the drunken man's recently deceased wife. The rough old fellow was melting. Soon, he was heard to say, "I don't got no wife. I don't got no home. I don't got no job. I'm so ashamed of myself." Tears rolled down his cheeks.

This peaceful resolution of the problem reminds us that there is an alternative to the violent confrontation that nearly occurred on the train. The drunken man's need to have power over others was a camouflage for his own hurts and needs. The same can be said of Laban. And that is true for many of the conflicts that occur in our families--even those we legitimate by calling them "customs."

For families who seek to live a Spirit-led, Christ-centered life, it would be wise to look behind the custom conflict and seek to discover the heart of the matter. If we look, we may discover practical solutions. Often, we will find hurts and fears that need to be healed and blessed by God. As we ask God to heal these places in our lives, may our family customs be lacking in conflict and be filled with moments that teach us we are truly blessed by God.

FOR DISCUSSION

1. What family customs or traditions are most important to you? Why are they important?

2. What family customs are most annoying or hurtful to you? Have you expressed this in non-threatening ways?

3. Can you identify areas where customs are clearly used as power mechanisms to control others?

4. Are there areas of recurring conflict in your family that might be lessened or resolved if the persons involved could calmly talk about their differences of opinion?

5. How does your family resolve conflict? What role does God have in this process?

Chapter 5

FORE!!

Genesis 4:1-16

It was a sunny, spring afternoon the day he swung a golf club as he had never swung it before. It may have been his first full stroke, though I am not certain. Since that memorable tee shot, he has driven many balls greater distances, but none has ever caused as much excitement as this one swing.

He was a friend of mine, a young boy then. He was the younger of two brothers. As was often the case, he and his older brother were spending the day playing outdoors. Romping through the brush and woods out back of their house was a frequent attraction. They played clumsy games of one-on-one at the dirt basketball court. Acquiring fresh grass stains in their clothes and decorating their flesh with an assortment of cuts and bruises as they wrestled and tumbled around the backyard was an added bonus.

The elder brother was not only older. He was taller, stronger and faster. When their activities turned competitive, as they usually did, it was the older boy who usually walked away victoriously. Despite their frequent competition, these siblings played together really well. This day had been no different in that regard--so far.

On this particular day, rather than basketball or wrestling, golf was the sport of choice even though there were no greens, holes or sandtraps in their front yard. What started out as a quiet, peaceful time together escalated into quite a confrontation. Perhaps the older brother began offering unwanted advice to his younger brother about how to hold the club, as older siblings are prone to do. Things like, "position your hands this way. Keep your arms in such and such position. Raise the club up and around behind you. When you swing, be sure to yell 'Fore!'" Maybe he was pestering his younger sibling, as only older brothers can do. Or perhaps his only crime that day was being in the wrong place at the wrong time. Whatever the reason, at some point that morning while the older brother was not looking, the younger sibling yelled--though I doubt he said "FORE!" As his voice spewed from his mouth like water exploding through a burst garden hose, he swung that club with all the power his little boy arms could muster.

The first thing the older brother heard was "THUD!" His next sensation was intense pain on the top of his head. He quickly became aware of two new sensations: the first was dizziness; the second was a warm, slow ooze working its way through his thick, sweat-matted hair down over his forehead. He dropped to the ground like a chunk of lead that had just discovered gravity. As he rolled on the grass sobbing with pain, his younger brother remained standing with the club raised, ready for another tee shot. Tears ran down his cheeks. With a pitch of voice that barely resembled his own, the younger boy was angrily threatening to do it again if necessary.

The younger of the two had always been the innovative athlete in the family, so this new twist on the game of golf should not have been a complete surprise. And though it is always good advice to "use your head," no one had ever suggested the older brother should pursue a career as a golf ball. His head was much too large for that. Plus, it was attached, which made long drives an impossibility.

After the tears had cleared and the stitches had been sewn, the family court convened. In his heart of hearts, the older brother was convinced he was innocent, and had done absolutely nothing to provoke or to merit such treatment. It had been a day like any other day. Anything he had said to his younger sibling regarding the use of the golf club was intended to be helpful. The younger brother, of course, had a different version of the story. In his view, his actions were provoked and deserved. The good news is that they both lived to tell about it. As adults, they are very close.

The sad news is that this is not one act limited to this family or this relationship. It is illustrative of what happens in many families. I am referring more to dynamics and patterns of relating than to historic first golf swings or open head wounds. There is a family fault line where rejection and devaluation occur, which in turn ignites angry retaliation.

People living in close quarters, physically or emotionally, frequently face potential eruptions like the one described above. The dynamics and results are similar; only the topics and instruments vary. For instance, we get tired of excessive instructions and know-it-all attitudes. We become weary from losing day after day after day at basketball, or at wrestling, or at work, or in domestic disputes, or wherever we expend our best effort. We grow fatigued from dealing with unsolicited advice, unnecessary comments, and unwanted commentary. These flammable contributions leak into the midst of common everyday encounters with family. Exhausted by a life which is demanding and unfair at times, family tempers are already simmering. Irritated by the people who perpetuate that facetious mode of living, those tempers can erupt at any time. As a result, many people find themselves teetering on the edge of an angry abyss.

The reason for this dangerous flirtation with anger is that certain combinations of factors take their toll on our well-being. The accumulation of unhelpful comments and ridiculing advice spawns feelings of inferiority, which in turn feeds feelings of worthlessness and rejection within the tenderest places of our hearts. The experience sets emotions churning, which swell like a raging sea, which in turn unleash the wave of anger which supplies the power that propels responses such as this historic first swing of a golf club.

That is what happened in the Biblical story about Cain and Abel. The story suggests that families were not in existence very long before squabbles of one type or another set in. We know the primary story line well. Two sons were born to Adam and Eve. They matured. In the course of time, each took an offering to God. God accepted Abel's offering but not Cain's.

Readers of the story have speculated for generations as to the reason for God's refusal of Cain's offering. It seems unfair, almost capricious. The frustrating truth is that the story is silent on that issue, though later Biblical writers understood it to be a matter of appropriate responses of faith: Abel's offering was; Cain's sacrifice was not. Whatever the reason for divine favoritism, Cain became furious. Even his face revealed his disappointment and anger. To settle the matter and to even the score, one day Cain invited Abel out to the field. Cain probably did not yell "FORE" before he took a historic first swing of his own, but Abel felt the blow. Unlike the case with my friends, there were no stitches after this family mishap. Only a funeral and, I suspect, a lot of heart-ache.

Our familiarity with this story may encourage us simply to shake our heads in dismay, and to resign ourselves to the fact that brothers will be brothers, or sisters will be sisters, or families will be families. However, if we read carefully, we discover the story teaches about a family fault located near instances of rejection, and the anger that infects the wounds associated with it.

Even the birth announcement of these two boys hints at the rejection issue. It reveals the affirmation received by one son but not by the other. The Scripture says, "Adam lay with his wife Eve and she conceived and gave birth to Cain. She said, 'With the help of the Lord I have brought forth a man.'" I imagine a lot of mothers have felt that way after a difficult birth! The story continues, "Later she gave birth to Abel." No grand exclamation accompanies the second child's entry into the world. There is no indication of this being a proud moment. It is just a routine mention that another child arrived.

In reality, that is not an unimaginable practice. Even though parents love all their children, most have to admit that with the birth of each successive child, the novelty decreases a bit. It is not that earlier children are more special than later ones. It is just that parents become more "seasoned veterans" with every additional birth. First-time parents have been known to go overboard with a birth video, baby's first book, bronzed shoes, enough toys to stock their own store, and oodles of studio-quality pictures perfectly labeled in photo albums. The mere thought of potential mishaps nearly paralyzes first-time parents, so that some firstborn infants are lucky to ever see the outdoors, to play in the mud, or to engage in other activities that could be remotely dangerous or dirty.

In contrast, the third and fourth children of some families are fortunate to have any pair of shoes not previously owned by one or more siblings or cousins. As for photos, other than school pictures, many later children are fortunate to have a handful of Polaroid snapshots. Even these are likely to be found stuffed inside an album, waiting to be labeled on a rainy day. As for safety and precaution, later siblings generally survive at least one "death-defying" stunt on a daily basis, often courtesy of their older siblings. Second, and third children, and so on, are no less loved. But they are never *first*, nor are they ever the *only* child. It all started with Adam and Eve.

The names of the brothers even imply one is valued over the other. The firstborn is named Cain, whose very name means "to create." But Abel's name means nothing so valiant. When the second child is born, he is called "vapor, vanity, nothingness." His name is from the same root used by the writer of Ecclesiastes when he exclaimed, "Vanity of vanities, all is vanity."[29] While Cain's name is the embodiment of vitality, Abel is almost dismissed.

Families can do little things, in most cases innocent things by intention and design, that send messages of rejection and devaluation to a person. Of course, at some point children must become responsible and work with God themselves, one-on-one in areas of self-esteem, self-worth, and personal happiness. Individuals should not be content to trudge along through life blaming their quirks and difficulties on others. Still, it would be nice to have a little assistance and support in the family arena.

Given the way the story begins, one would expect that Abel would have been the one who eventually exploded over the angry edge. Interestingly enough, it was Cain--Mr. Vitality himself--who cracked. Cain and Abel each offered a sacrifice to God. Both had reason to anticipate acceptance and affirmation. For reasons known to God alone, only Abel's sacrifice--and thus only Abel--was accepted. And Cain . . . was . . . livid!

All these years as the family had inadvertently overvalued Cain and devalued Abel, it seems that Cain had grown comfortable determining his worth through favorable comparisons with his brother. That is a fatal mistake. If we teach that lesson in our families, we are sending a gold-lettered invitation requesting that disaster move in as a permanent house guest. When the moment came that Abel was recognized and honored as a person acceptable to God rather than as a vaporous nothing, Mr. Vitality could not handle it.

Later, God's conversation with Cain really takes us to the crux of the matter. It may seem unfair, but rejection in life does occur. The question is, "What do we do once it happens?" God told Cain that as he dealt with this rejection, in this moment of anger "sin was crouching at the door . . . and it was his responsibility to master it." That is not to imply that anger is sinful; but sometimes what we do with our anger is. In this case, unfortunately sin won the round, and Abel lost his life. Cain's feelings of rejection incited anger, which led to violence and retaliation. That is the unhealthy family pattern this Scripture illuminates and helps eliminate.

The reality to which we are alerted is that on some level, every rejection is real, even if in perception only. A family member who feels she is the "throw away" or "black sheep," even if that is not the case, needs to be convinced otherwise. The one who thinks he can never measure up to his father's standards, even if the thought is incorrect, must be assured that he is appreciated on his own terms. Perception, even if inaccurate, is powerful.

Unfortunately many family rejections are not imagined or hidden. Where I was raised, it used to be customary to send unwed mothers away "temporarily" because they were pregnant out of wedlock. It seems to have been a way of dealing with family honor and embarrassment. I still remember a pregnant teenager who "mysteriously disappeared" one year when I was in elementary school. We were told she had gone to Florida to visit relatives. Perhaps she did. Wherever she went, she was no longer pregnant when she returned. But neither did she have the child with her. Though I have never heard her speak of it, I can only imagine the rejection and anger that were involved in that incident.

Other messages of family rejection are more subtle. The sentence, "This is our gifted child" may well be a true statement, but the implication is that the other children are not gifted. Some messages are nonverbal. The choice to spend extreme amounts of time with a job, or people other than our spouses or children, sends a clear communication about our feelings toward family. Or reminders to our parents of just how much of an inconvenience it is to visit or call when we have more important things to do sends more of a message than we may be aware. The rejection may or may not be intentional, but that does not make the effect any less real. When rejection is common, we can expect anger to be a frequent visitor in our homes.

The book *Jacob the Baker* contains a story about a man who went into the bakery where Jacob worked. Jacob made a practice of placing written tidbits of wisdom in the bread he baked. On this day, the man entering the bakery was waving one of the messages he found in his loaf of bread. "What do you mean by this?" he asked, and he proceeded to read, "The fist starves the hand."

Jacob took all the man's anger, consumed its force, and transformed it, returning peace in his voice and manner. He replied, "When our hand is made into a fist, we cannot receive the gifts of life from ourselves, our friends, or our God. When our hand is closed in a fist, we cannot hold anything but our bitterness. When we do this, we starve our stomachs and our souls. Our anger brings a famine on ourselves."[30] I would add that famine of this type affects our families as well, particularly along the lines of this family fault.

The story of Cain and Abel actually exposes a triad of faults, all lying closely together. The first is the possibility of promoting feelings of rejection by appearing to devalue a person. The second is basing one's self-esteem and sense of self-worth on how we compare with other people instead of who we are before God. The third fault area is destructive anger that responds to rejection by means of retaliation.

As for the final fault, we need to understand that anger is basically an intent to preserve personal worth, essential needs, and fundamental convictions. It is usually wrapped around issues of self-esteem, power, and rejection like honeysuckle along a fence, only not nearly as pretty and lacking its sweet fragrance. Anger can be a positive instrument for change and growth in a relationship when it is controlled by love and by an awareness of the other person's worth and rights. But often, that is not how the scenario ends. Instead, anger assumes a much more damaging role and becomes a destructive family force.

Though the opening story of this chapter was about young boys, rejection and anger are not limited to children. Though the Scripture story is about brothers, this fault line is not limited to males or sibling relationships. Though an act of physical aggression occurred in each story, we should not assume that if there is no physical violence in our family that rejection and anger do not live under our roofs. When intimacy and sharing cease, rejection and anger may have formed a tag team. When silence is present but is not golden, rejection and anger may be haunting the halls of our homes.

When withdrawal and depression are common, rejection and anger may be present. When these things dominate our family relationships, love and happiness will seem really scarce.

The bad news is that even the best of families and the best of lives experience moments of rejection. Those moments *will* come. Anger may well follow. The good news is, God says that we do not have to sin in those moments. We can learn to master anger and channel it. That is how God instructed Cain to cope with the situation. I suspect the same Divine Advice would be given today, were we to ask.

As families, we can begin to overcome this fault by learning to value rather than to devalue other persons. We can calm the tremors in this area by intentionally sending messages of affirmation rather than messages of rejection. As individuals, we contribute to healing by learning to be angry without sinning. We can begin by looking often to the grace and instruction of God, so that our feelings of rejection can be soothed and our anger mastered. In the meantime, keep a close watch on any golf clubs in your house, and learn to duck when someone yells "FORE!"

FOR DISCUSSION

1. Is it permissible to get angry in your family, or are subtle psychological mechanisms such as "the silent treatment" employed to dissuade the expression of anger?

2. Do you unintentionally (or intentionally) reject or demean members in your family by words or actions? Why does it seem necessary to deal with them in this manner?

3. Do you feel that members of your family do not appreciate or respect you? Have you expressed this to them?

4. Are there any family relationships currently strained because of anger? How long has this been the case?

5. What are the means of reconciliation within your family? Does everyone understand the "family approved" method for resolving angry disputes?

Chapter 6

EUCHRED!!
II SAMUEL 11

Part of my initiation into Midwestern culture and my wife's family included learning to play a card game called Euchre. Until we met, I had never before heard of such a pastime. Rummy, Rook, and Uno were familiar friends. Many good study hours in college were wasted playing Spades. I was no stranger to card games, but I had never, ever heard of Euchre. In fact no one I have ever met who lacks an Indiana connection is familiar with it either. Yet for some Hoosiers, not knowing how to play Euchre amounts to being culturally-deprived.

The game was introduced to me when Judi's grandparents came to visit during her student days at Duke Divinity School. A favorable introduction was important, since this was the first of those family introductions that must occur somewhere during the courtship process. Euchre was a safe, suitable activity, providing a low-pressure forum within which we could become acquainted.

Having now learned to play the game fairly well, (and thus, having acquired some culture), it has since become apparent that no two families seem to play the same way. My earliest exposure was to regular trump euchre. Next I was introduced to bid euchre. Later, someone taught me six handed euchre, played with two decks. I learned about "alone" hands and the names for them. Alone hands are often called "shooting the moon." In Judi's family, they are referred to as "little horse" and "big horse." A "little horse" means swapping one card with your partner and playing an alone hand, worth twelve points. A "big horse" means playing an alone hand without swapping a card, worth twenty-four points. And through trial, error, and poor judgment, I learned about being euchred, which refers to going set and losing points for not making one's bid. Getting euchred really hurts when the bid is a little horse or a big horse because it subtracts twelve or twenty-four points from the score.

Once Judi's grandpa and I were losing by a wide margin. In fact we were in the hole with a substantial negative number. After yet another losing hand for us, Judi announced the score--it was eighteen to minus thirty. I said to her grandpa, "Well, Grandpa, we're just a couple of big horses behind." To which my ever supportive wife immediately replied, "You sure are!" (I've yet to see the resemblance.)

We visit her grandparents often. They are in the autumn years of their lives and it is important to make the most of the opportunities we have with them. When we see them, this game is always played. Over the countless games we've shared, it has become apparent that Euchre has become more than a game of cards. Beneath the level of bidding, playing, and being euchred, important family work occurs. We catch up on the latest news. We share about plans for vacation, or redecorating, or shopping trips. We learn what is happening in each other's lives. The real stuff that helps families bond and stay healthy takes place in the background beneath the game.

Over time, as we have taken care of family business, I have had a chance to learn a lot about euchre. A person can play the game in a couple of ways. One can be a solid role player who never overbids, will usually supplement his or her partner, and will occasionally have an outstanding hand. In such a case, a team doesn't make quick, outstanding gains, but they are seldom euchred either.

Or, rather than a role player, one can be a bit of a gambler. This person will almost always overbid. A gambler hopes and prays the cards fall right. He or she counts on the partner to come through in the clutch if necessary. In short, this type of player is a risk-taker--one who bluffs--and one who will likely go set on occasion. If you are a gambler, you have to accept the fact that there will be times when you hear the other team triumphantly proclaim "euchre."

The fact that the score of our game was eighteen to minus thirty gives you an idea of what kind of euchre player I have become. I was a role player for a while. Since it is just a card game, I eventually became a risk-taker. But it *is* just a card game. Even so it is amazing to watch what happens when someone is euchred. When that occurs, it momentarily steals everyone's attention. The family business being taken care of on one level is invariably interrupted while the winner gloats, teases, and taunts over the euchre. When the excitement finally dies down, we are able to move on to the next hand and more importantly, back to family business. But we have to stop and ask, "Where were we with the conversation? What were we talking about?" Being euchred temporarily interrupts the important stuff of life and throws us out of sync.

This card game scenario is useful for thinking about family relationships. We do not necessarily sit around a card table, but we do live together. As we do, we must find ways to take care of our family business. It includes such things as communication, listening, jobs, support, all of which are needed to build and to maintain healthy families. While we participate in these areas, we are also involved in another sphere. Specifically, I am referring to those areas of involvement outside the immediate family context. These include our friendships, our hobbies, our work, and our community contributions, to name a few.

In those realms, as in euchre, we choose what type of participant we will be. Sometimes, we select the option of role player. We make sensible decisions and live supportive lives. Or, instead of being the role player who allows the family business to occur without interruption, a person may become a gambler. He or she begins to bluff about his or her potential situation, such as who they are, what they can give and what they wish to receive. That person begins to take unhealthy risks at the expense of the family. Sometimes those bluffs involve a person in things in which he or she should not be involved. And sometimes, the gamblers will get euchred. It is the same concept as the card game, but to an elevated degree with higher stakes. In this realm of life, the consequences are much more costly.

The simple name for this family fault is infidelity. Within the family context, that term usually refers to sexual infidelity. That is an important issue in today's family, no doubt. As a conveyor of cultural values, television and cinema illustrate the ease with which such choices are made today, as well as their frequency. In no way is this form of infidelity to be minimized as an active family fault. However, it is important to understand at the outset that not all infidelity is sexual in nature. It occurs wherever and in whatever ways we are unfaithful to our families and to their best interest. It can involve our allocation of time to our home life. It can entail the manner in which we invest our finances and our energy in positive ways for the family. It can include the manner in which we are present spiritually and emotionally for those we love and for whom we have some responsibility.

A Scripture story that provides guidance on this topic is probably one of the best known stories from the era of King David's reign. A careful reader will notice that something is amiss in verse one which reads, "in the spring, at the time when kings go off to war, David sent Joab out with the king's men and the whole Israelite army. They destroyed the Ammonites and besieged Rabbah. But David remained in Jerusalem." The Israelites had wanted a king to lead them into battle. That, after all, is one of the things kings do according to verse one. However on this occasion, rather than valiantly leading his soldiers into the fight, David sent someone else to do it. He stayed home. While others waged the fight for the preservation of the kingdom, behind the battle lines David lounged in a safe, peaceful haven. Something is amiss in this story!

One evening as David lounged safely on the palace roof top, he saw a beautiful woman by the name of Bathsheba. The story does not waste time with suspense, or even a moral dilemma. It does not even provide details. Instead, the story reports a sequence of events in rapid fashion. David saw Bathsheba. He sent for her. She came to him. They slept together. Bathsheba returned home.

If this had been a euchre game, David would have just overestimated his hand and bid more than he could cover. He thought that being king placed all the trumps in his hand. But when Bathsheba sent word she was pregnant as a result of their rendezvous, it is not inaccurate to say that David had been euchred. He definitely went set.

An act of infidelity sets this story in motion. Bathsheba was unfaithful to her husband Uriah. She may have felt she had no choice when the king's messenger knocked on her door. Or perhaps she was a willing participant. We do not know. David, too, was unfaithful. Even if the Hebrew culture justified his having more than one wife, it did not justify a relationship with another man's wife. In this one act, David managed to violate two of the commandments which were foundational in the Israelite covenant. He coveted his neighbor's wife, and he committed adultery. Moreover, in violating the covenant, David was unfaithful to God, raising the broken commandment total to three. As a member of the covenant community, as the king no less, his duty was to honor the covenant with God and the expectations it created for human relationships. The severity of his sin in this area is illustrated by the prophet Nathan's parable in chapter twelve.

Their act of infidelity was a problem in and of itself. But the situation was compounded by what followed, namely deceit. As a cover up, David feigned interest in Bathsheba's husband, a soldier named Uriah. (Imagine how it must have felt to Uriah for the king to take such interest in his well being!) Of course, deceit never acts alone. For deceit to occur, trust must be broken. So David, this king whom Uriah trusted, deceived his faithful soldier. He betrayed Uriah's trust. David invited him home from the battle front for a bit of R & R. He encouraged Uriah to a state of intoxication in hopes of sending him home to Bathsheba, where a close encounter of the intimate kind would solve the King's dilemma. He and Bathsheba could then claim the child was Uriah's.

But David underestimated Uriah's honor and his loyalty to his king and country. He refused to spend time with his wife while his fellow countrymen were at war. In contrast to David's deceit and infidelity the story presents us with Uriah's strong moral character. Surprised by this soldier's faithfulness, and running out of options, David ordered Uriah placed on the front line in the heat of the battle, where Uriah was quickly killed. What started out as a risky hand ended in a euchre. What started out as an unfaithful act of personal gratification destroyed a family.

This affair and its effects all occur in the everyday arena of human interactions. It is not a particularly religious story. We read nothing of God's location or perspective in the account. Yet when the prophet Nathan later rebuked David,[31] God said to the king through the prophet that, in this act of infidelity, "You despised me." That statement reminds us that these were covenant people. All the affairs of daily living (no pun intended) fell within the boundaries of their relationship with God. That ultimate relationship should order their associations and partnerships with other people in ways that honor family commitments.

This story highlights the family fault of infidelity, which stands in stark contrast to commitment. It contains lessons for us to learn as heirs of the Israelite tradition and keepers of the New Covenant. The David-Bathsheba episode demonstrates that unfaithfulness is linked to issues of trust and betrayal. The outcome of the story teaches us that when this principle is active in our families, it will interrupt the love, care and stability that should permeate our homes. As Uriah's demise showed, if left unchecked, infidelity has the potential to wreck our families completely.

Infidelity of a sexual nature within the confines of marriage is certainly a problem in our society. Many television shows and movies portray it as natural and acceptable. No matter how much families and churches try to teach a monogamous set of standards, the impact of the media on morals and relationships can hardly be overestimated. This is a major contributor to the family fault known as infidelity. Regardless of how we justify such an act, it represents a breaking of a covenant with God and spouse. We need to pray for families who are in such situations, and for a nation that encourages it.

But infidelity is not limited to sexual situations. The fault of infidelity lies near wherever we see ourselves being unfaithful to the things which make for a healthy family. We can speak of emotional infidelity, if accepting, caring, intimate family ties are lacking. We can talk of spiritual infidelity if we do not create homes that demonstrate faith and encourage it among others. It can apply to child-rearing, if parents are not faithful to the family by investing the time and the compassion that creates a positive, stable, nurturing home environment. It can apply to putting forth the necessary effort to keep communication lines open or to resolve conflicts. It is probably beginning to sound like infidelity was a simpler, safer subject when it was just about sexual misconduct. This broadened perspective makes family life seem demanding. Truthfully, it *is* more than co-habitating, wearing a ring, and giving birth!

The pastor of a large, city church ran an ad for a caretaker/housekeeper. The next day, a well-dressed young man appeared at the pastor's door. The pastor immediately began questioning him. "Can you sweep? Can you make beds, shovel walks, run errands, fix meals, balance a checkbook, and baby-sit?" he asked. The young man replied, "Just hold on a minute. I came to see about getting married. If it's that much work, I'm not interested." The truth is, marriage and family are that much work! Only the naive and uninitiated can persist in believing that having a family is easy and free of effort.

When Jesus spoke of the family, he quoted the Genesis passage that speaks of a husband and wife clinging to each other. Hugging and holding sound easy. Clinging sounds like work, complete with tense fingers and aching muscles. It implies laboring against forces that push for separation and division.

Also, through Paul we are taught that the quality of and commitments to the family relationship need to emulate those that exist between Christ and the church. We need to understand that fidelity, commitment and trust, along with a little difficulty and effort, are built into family.

Long ago in a now forgotten source, I read of a person on a plane flying home from a conference. Over the course of the trip, one particular flight attendant had been quite friendly, even flirtatious. As the flight neared completion, the attendant, who had a two-day layover, suggested they spend some time together.

Without hesitation the passenger said, "No thanks. I'm married."

The attendant was surprised at the quick response and said, "Who do you think you are? Don't you at least want to think about it?"

The passenger replied simply, "There's nothing to think about. It's not because of who I am. It is because I know what I am: faithful and committed to my family. End of story!"

Maybe that response sounds too idealistic to be realistic. Perhaps it sounds too syrupy for real life. But that is the clinging to which Christ referred. It is the commitment Paul described. It is the missing element in the story of David and Bathsheba. Through the grace and strength of God, it is the kind of fidelity we can offer to our families. Though it may demand a bit of work, it surely will reduce the probability of our families getting euchred.

FOR DISCUSSION

1. How does infidelity affect your household?

2. Think about your investment in your family. Are you best described as a role player or a gambler? What are the advantages and disadvantages of each role?

3. Are there any current events or issues that are interrupting the love and stability of your home?

4. What activities provide opportunities for your family to bond and exchange crucial information? Name ways you can improve the situation.

Chapter 7

USED PEOPLE
GENESIS 15:1-6 & 16:1-5

You are probably familiar with the fairy tale "The Princess and the Pea." A creative author has retold it as "The Princess and the Bowling Ball." A summary of his revised version helps introduce the focus of this chapter.

Once upon a time there was a Prince. And this Prince's dad and mom, like many parents, decided no princess would be good enough for their boy unless she could feel a pea through one hundred mattresses.

Needless to say, the Prince had a very hard time finding a princess. Every time he met a nice girl, his mom and dad would pile one hundred mattresses on top of a pea and then invite her to sleep over. On the next morning when the Queen would ask, "How did you sleep, dear?" the Princess would politely say, "Fine, thank you." The King would then promptly dismiss her.

This went on for three years, with nobody ever feeling the pea under one hundred mattresses. One day the Prince met the girl of his dreams and decided to take matters into his own hands. That night, before the Princess went to bed, he slipped his bowling ball under the one hundred mattresses.

When the Princess came down for breakfast the next morning, the Queen asked, "How did you sleep, dear?"

The Princess answered, "This might sound odd, but I think you need another mattress. I felt like I was sleeping on a lump as big as a bowling ball."

The King and Queen were satisfied. The Prince and Princess were married. And everyone lived happily, though maybe not completely honestly, ever after.[32]

That may sound like a fairly stupid tale instead of a fairy tale, but there are many families in which this could be a fairly true tale, in principle if not in actual content. Even the best of families have their share of controlling, domineering personalities intent on choreographing the lives of their loved ones like the director of a made-for-TV mini-series. The interference runs over a wide gamut. It may arise in frequent negative comments about one's habits and preferences, assuredly given for the improvement of the beloved. It may focus on disapproving of every potential mate introduced to the family, supposedly so that a person saves himself or herself from a wrong choice and a resulting life of misery. It may discourage an individual from risking new challenges, or learning new hobbies, under the guise of not wanting a loved one to be taken advantage of or to become over-stressed. As the choreography is revealed, it comes with an insistence that the controlling family member has only the other's best interest in mind. In reality, they are serving or protecting their own interests. For whatever reason, these individuals feel overly responsible for the happiness and well-being of others, and set up controlled situations designed to produce the desired results. In such situations, the Prince's response in the story is not an uncommon one. As people grow tired of the interference and decide to take charge of their lives, they look for ways to circumvent those domineering plans. They strive to find a way to live happily, though not necessarily honestly, ever after.

When that sort of scenario is present, family relationships often degenerate into a series of manipulative ploys that have one common denominator: they use people. Most people like to feel useful; but few of us want to discover we are being used. The difference is this: *useful* is when we have the ability to make a contribution and choose to do so. *Being used* is when others recognize we can make a contribution to their plans and draws upon our talents. Even then, being used can be a positive thing.

When I was about to turn sixteen and receive my driver's license, my mother informed me that she intended to use my newly-acquired status to help lighten her load by sending me on errands. I was delighted to be used in that manner. What sixteen-year-old does not dream of being turned loose, alone in a car, on a wide-open highway with a full tank of gas. "Gee, you look tired, mom. Why don't you stay home and rest? I can drive to town and get the groceries. Maybe you'd like a bucket of sand fresh off the beach. It is only three hours away. I will bring back a few shells for you, too."

Being used occurs when someone recognizes we can make a contribution and draws upon our talents. However, when one's contribution is demanded without permission or input, misuse occurs. When our contribution is demanded without permission *and* without any thought for the negative consequences such actions have on us, abuse usually rears its ugly head. When families thrive on using each other instead of loving each other, we live on one of the shakiest of faults, begging for an earthquake to shatter our worlds.

The Genesis story chosen for this chapter gives us a window into the dynamics of the family fault where used people congregate. In God and Abram's conversation, God promised to bless Abram's life. Old Testament rewards and blessings were primarily perceived to be material in nature, particularly in the form of wealth, land and offspring. Abram responded to God, "What can you give me since I remain childless?"

The frustration behind Abram's question to God may be paraphrased as such: "if your goal is to make my name great, nothing you can give me matters since there is no family other than Sara and I to receive it. There is no one to receive such an inheritance. None of this matters without family. Without family, my name will be forgotten by the next generation." God responded with a promise that, indeed, this couple would have a child.

This encounter reveals that having a family was an ultimate priority for Abram and Sara. We also learn that God promised to help them create a family. With that knowledge, we begin reading chapter sixteen. There, we discover that after ten years of waiting and no "loaves in the oven," Sara approached Abram with a plan. She had decided to give him her maidservant, Hagar. Abram and Hagar would have a child on Sara's behalf.

The idea of "giving" someone to someone else probably sounds strange to us, as it implies ownership or subservience of some type. Ours is a culture where past acceptance of the practice of slavery still creates twinges of guilt, shame and anger in the collective conscience of society. We live in an era where Western thought promotes individual sovereignty and freedom, almost to an extreme. The very idea of Sara being in a position to give her maidservant to her husband is strange to us indeed. Archaeological evidence from that time period suggests this was an acceptable custom for childless families in Semitic cultures. Even so, regardless of the era, I doubt it ever feels very good or affirming to be given, swapped, or traded like baseball cards or melons in a fruit market. But that was Sara's plan.

No sooner was the gift given than Hagar conceived. Finally! A child was on the way. Abram and Sara's family would be perpetuated after all! They would have an heir to receive the abundant inheritance made possible by God's blessings. But rather than finding joy and fulfillment in this new development, Sara felt distant from and betrayed by her husband and servant. Hagar apparently had problems with the arrangement as well. The text says Hagar began to despise her mistress.

The manipulative dynamics within this story cry out to be noticed. The problem began when the couple's fears, needs, and desires were combined with a lack of trust in and patience with God. That is understandable enough. Many a prayer has been prayed in Eastern Standard Time, only to discover God's watch is set to a much later time zone. Probably none of us does not know what it is like to be impatient, or to wish God would synchronize the divine Big Ben with our own personal wristwatches. As a solution to their dilemma, Abram and Sara decided (and perhaps we have done this, too, at times) to try to fulfill their dreams themselves. Perhaps that is okay as well, for we have often been told that "God helps those who help themselves--who put forth some effort--who show some initiative." But the practical truth is that faithful living is sort of like ballroom dancing. It goes smoothest if we remember who is leading. Unfortunately, those who try to be hasty *and* faithful sometimes confuse following a Divine leading with trying to lead a following, which is something like trying to tango while our partner is waltzing.

From the perspective of family fault lines, the real problem here is that, rather than trusting God or even themselves, Abram and Sara decided to fulfill their dreams by using someone else. It is a similar scenario to that of parents trying to relive their childhood fantasies through their own children, brutally pushing them to excel in Little League, insisting they choose the career the parents wish they had chosen, or using pea-under-the-mattress criteria to screen prospective daughters-in-law and sons-in-law. Abram and Sara's plan is like that used by children who refuse to grow up, always expecting their parents to rescue them, to send them money, to raise their children, and to solve all their problems.

Using people in itself is destructive enough, but the worst is yet to come. When these manipulative ploys do not bring the satisfaction expected (and the truth is they cannot bring it), then the general tendency is to blame the person we have used for the mess we have created and for the grief it has caused us.

That is exactly what happened in Abram and Sara's household. With the pregnancy came a child, which the couple wanted. But since there was no happiness, Sara blamed Abram and mistreated Hagar. Abram tried to wash his hands of any responsibility in the matter. Meanwhile Hagar ran away, preferring to die than to live this used, misused, abused life. If their story is feeling a little uncomfortable, it is probably because it sounds familiar. It is quite possible that we have been a player in some version of this scenario.

I watched a movie recently involving a family full of used people. It involved a rich uncle, worth about $25 million, and a horde of inheritance-seeking nephews and nieces. The uncle was an expert in using his money as a tool to keep his relatives showing up at family gatherings, offering ridiculous tokens of their false affections, and jockeying for position in the inheritance sweepstakes. The nieces and nephews all actually hated the uncle, but they performed like circus acts whenever they thought there was a chance of increasing the sum of their inheritance. It was a pitiful display of greed and manipulation.

As the plot progressed, we viewers learned that the uncle had been abandoned at a county home by his mother. As a result of that experience, he didn't think anyone could love him for who he was. That is why he manipulated his family with money. It was all a sad effort to create a family, secure the love which could make him feel valuable, and convince himself that his life had been worthwhile. That is not so far from the scenario in our Scripture story, and perhaps in many of our own families.

If we listen closely to the story, we begin to discover the reason for this sort of behavior. What appears to be manipulation, domination, and even greed within family relations, is often merely an attempt to "create" the family we want and need in order to feel like we are "worthy" or like "we matter." It is all an effort to create for ourselves what we know God has promised us, but which we do not completely trust God to help us create.

Shortly after arriving in New Castle, Indiana, where I currently reside, I called on all our church members who lived in health care facilities. At one of these places, a woman in a wheelchair asked if I would get a seat cushion for her. Her seat was hard, and sitting in it hours at a time was uncomfortable. She said the cushions were on the linen cart by the nurses' station. Though I have seen pillow cushions, bleacher cushions and an occasional whoopee cushion, it was not obvious to me which items on that cart were cushions, so I inquired at the nurses' station about their availability. They looked at me like I was crazy. There were no cushions on that cart, I was informed. Just towels and bed sheets and such.

Red-faced, feeling manipulated, suckered, like a fool, and vowing never to trust the judgment of strangers in a health care facility again, I apologetically relayed the message that no such cushion was available. Our conversation moved to other topics.

Nearly three years later as I turned the hall corner in that same facility, I nearly fell on top of a little woman who was bent over by the linen cart. She was folding some piece of material into a square to serve as a cushion for the hard seat in her wheel chair. The nurses may not know it, but there are cushions on that linen cart!

I chuckled at the sight, and even felt slightly ashamed for jumping to conclusions regarding the resident who had originally asked me for a cushion. I realized that although I had felt a bit like those manipulated, used people described above, the truth of the matter is that people are not always out to trick us or to control us. Often, they are unaware of it. The truth is they are probably doing the best they can with who they are and what they understand in that particular moment.

The grandparent who simultaneously insists you take second and third helpings at the dinner table, yet reminds you that you are gaining weight probably is not aware of the contradiction in behavior or of the reason weight seems like such an important issue. The spouse who vehemently disagrees with a mate's desire to return to school may not be aware that fear of change or separation is the real reason for resisting the idea. In many cases, controlling family members are trying to take care of themselves the only way they know how.

That is the saddest part of this scenario--that they (we) do not know a better way. Ignorance of the practice does not make using people justified, acceptable, or even tolerable. In fact, it is often necessary to firmly but lovingly confront such manipulative and negative behaviors. However, it should be remembered that grace and compassion are in order, even as we attempt to find ways to stop the use and abuse.

The good news in the story is that God finds a way to heal, to recycle, to rebuild and to reuse used people. God found the runaway Hagar and promised to bless her and her child. God also found a way to reassure Abram and Sara that, if patient, they would have the family they wanted and needed. And they did.

If you have been used and abused, God can heal the fractures this fault has caused in your life, too. This story teaches us about learning to trust God. The promises and potential of life should be fulfilled within the parameters of God's timing, not ours.

This story also illustrates that healthy families should help each other grow in love, trust and confidence. For without these three essential ingredients, a family will never have a very happy home. So long as they are absent, family members will likely feel a need to control what they cannot trust, and to succeed vicariously where they themselves have failed.

If the grace of God is to heal this family fault, we need to be useful to one another without using one another. We all have contributions we can make, gifts we can share. But a family of willing participants is always preferable to one of coerced contributors. Simply put, we must learn that the promises of God and the mutual cooperation of family are always more useful than bowling balls and peas.

FOR DISCUSSION

1. How has God blessed your family? Are there some blessings you believe should be yours, but are not yet?

2. Is control an issue in your family? If so, where is this most evident?

3. In what ways would you like to be most useful to your family?

4. Can you name times when you have felt used by other family members, without your consent?

5. How can you trust God more and control others less?

Chapter 8

PROMISE BREAKERS
II Samuel 13:1-22

People in Indiana are enterprising folks. I recently passed a barn serving double duty as a bill board. Even as the building housed livestock or stored hay, it advertised the products of a brand name company. That is not an unfamiliar site in this area. In fact, when my wife was a little girl, her dad once pointed to a barn and told her that is where she was born. The building to which he pointed had a tobacco advertisement on one side. Barns with that particular logo were scattered around the countryside. For a while after that, every time my wife saw a barn with that particular sign, she would wonder how she managed to be born in so many places!

This particular advertisement captured my attention because the logo it bore was a familiar one. It represented a livestock feed company. When I saw it, I immediately flashed back twenty years ago to the day a representative of that feed company came to our little dairy farm in North Carolina. The company was new in the area and he was canvasing the neighborhood, calling on all the potential customers. As you can imagine, according to him, he had the feed of our dreams. This was the *ABSOLUTE MOTHER* of all dairy feeds. He showed literature boasting of increased milk production in dairy herds as a result of their feed. A neighbor of ours had switched to it a month ago and experienced similar results, he said. The salesman offered a guaranteed analysis of the feed, and it was impressive. He pointed out ways in which his feed was superior to the formula used by our current feed company. We would be pleased with their products and service, he promised. Imagine the AT&T/MCI/Sprint long distance war applied to agricultural services, and you will get an accurate picture of the situation.

After awhile, a person becomes accustomed to those kinds of sales pitches and never takes them at face value. So a farmer in the community sent a sample of the feed to a nearby laboratory to have it analyzed. Lo and behold, it was every bit as good as the salesman had claimed! So we, and a lot of farmers in the area, made the switch.

The first couple of months after the switch, things went just as the salesman said they would. Milk production all over the county increased, which meant more money and higher profits. There were a lot of happy farmers in our area those two months. But not long afterwards, things began to change. Production dropped. Oh, the animals were still chugging away, eating like it was their last meal. The feed was going in, but the milk was not coming out. Money was being lost. Happy farmers became a rare commodity.

All over the county, questions began to be raised. Concerns were expressed. Complaints were registered. Finally different farmers had feed samples analyzed. They discovered that the analysis had been changed. They were being given a lower grade feed. Oh, the ticket still boasted the same guaranteed analysis, but in reality, promises were being broken. As a result, people--good, trusting people who were living up to their end of the bargain--were being exploited.

It is a sad world where people fail to honor their word and care for the trusts that are given to them. But that is a major component of reality as we know it. What that means in real, historical terms is that many relationships, whether personal or business, are filled with abuse and neglect. We do not have to look for subtle examples because painfully blatant ones surround us.

Wedding day vows promising to love and to honor a spouse are sometimes forgotten, leading to the neglect of the marriage covenant and the eventual disintegration of the relationship. High profile trials involving celebrities raise many questions about spousal abuse in the form of battering and violence. Headlines shove in our faces one horrifying story after another of a parent's neglect and violation of a child's trust.

The news overflows with examples. Statistics are staggering as well. Recent studies state that three children die each day as a result of abuse or neglect, while an estimated 100,000 U.S. children are homeless each day. It is possible that some of these situations may be next door to us, or down the street, or even in our own families. Just thinking of it can reduce one to tears. The tragic fact is, it is an old problem.

The story contained in II Samuel 13 is one that knows about abuse and neglect. It is a sad story, one that perhaps we shudder to see contained within the pages of Scripture, but one that is no doubt included for a purpose. The setting is the royal household. Specifically, it involves Amnon, Tamar and Absalom, all of whom are children of King David.

The good news is that Amnon has fallen in love. The bad news is that the object of his affections is his half-sister Tamar. The Scripture says he became frustrated to the point of illness, which should clue us in that something is wrong with this love. When we pay close attention to how he interacted with others, we discover that Amnon was one who instructed and ordered, but seldom listened, except to those who helped him get his way. He grabbed and used force to get what he wanted. That, it seems, is a very accurate description of the manner of relating that occurs among those who tend to neglect or abuse others in some way. Abuse takes without asking. It threatens, intimidates, and strikes for the sheer pleasure of it all. Domination and fear are its greatest allies.

Amnon only listened to the advice of one person in this story, a shrewd fellow named Jonadab. Jonadab had a small part in the account, but he was involved just enough to be a catalyst. He supported Amnon's frustrations to the point of devising a scheme for him. By his selectivity of friends, Amnon surrounded himself with people who reinforced and promoted his sick wishes. That is one way abusive persons preserve their power and deny their problem. They attempt to eliminate critical and contradictory points of view in favor of like minds and those who only answer "yes," regardless of the question.

Amnon's desires, reinforced by Jonadab's scheme, cast a net that seemed to catch Tamar completely off guard. Tamar is a fairly passive character in the story. She trusted Amnon's words, doing as she was instructed without question until his motives became apparent. As Tamar pleaded with her half-brother not to force himself upon her, she asked a most revealing question--one that is ignored by promise breakers such as Amnon: "What about me? Where could I get rid of my disgrace?" Perhaps that is the worst impact of neglect and abuse. It dumps the victim into a pool of disgrace, infested with shame and swirling with feelings of worthlessness.

Tamar was actually willing to give herself to Amnon, fulfilling his love, if only he would pursue her along proper channels. She said, "Speak to the king. He will not keep me from being married to you." Unfortunately, people who promote neglect and abuse are seldom interested in others. They care nothing about the effect of their actions on their victims. They are concerned with fulfilling personal desires to the point that draining the life energy from someone else is of no consequence to them.

So, Amnon raped his sister Tamar, and then he hated her. As is so often the case for those who neglect and abuse others, the things taken seldom satisfy the abuser's real needs. Thus the person goes away disappointed, even hateful, leaving a trail strewn with pain and destruction. And true to form, Amnon sent Tamar away, compounding wrong upon wrong.

A third child of the king, Absalom, tried to help in his own way, but failed. He took Tamar to live in his house. This was a good, caring thing to do. It provided a refuge, a safe place for Tamar. But Absalom told his sister not to take the horrible event to heart, which was a nearly impossible request. Plus, even as he gave such misguided advice, he himself could not help but take it to heart. He began to hate his brother and plotted Amnon's murder. Thus, the abusive behavior of Amnon left Tamar broken, set off Absalom's short fuse, and eventually brought death to Amnon himself. Abuse leads to hatred, which, if left unchecked, can turn to retaliation and vengeance. The whole process becomes circular and self-perpetuating.

This is a tragic story contained in Scripture. The worse calamity is that promise breakers are not limited to ancient cultures and past generations. Within families, neglect and abuse occur between persons who are supposedly intimate and loving. Neglect and abuse come in all shapes and forms. They may be verbal, emotional, or physical. They can result from a poor choice of words or no words at all. They may be inflicted by hatred's venom, by a sick or misguided love, or even by a good love inadequately expressed. They can be delivered with blows of physical violence, inappropriate touches, or from affectionate touches withheld. They happen in a society that ignores the hurts of its people, and in families that are too busy to take care of their own. They can be the end result of no standards, inadequate standards or too rigid standards. They can prey on any age group, from the youngest to the oldest. Any class of people--from the richest to the poorest--is susceptible to its ravages. As we read the story and think about our own society, we cannot help but ask, "Where was and is God in all of this?"

It is interesting that God is not mentioned in this story. The narrative is completely silent about God's presence or response. That is powerfully symbolic! Promise breakers desire a silent God, at least while victimizing others. Promise breakers do not want to know what God requires in a situation because knowledge of God's will can only emphasize their wrong and demand their repentance. Conscious knowledge of what is right will only intensify one's sense of being wrong.

We might also ask how could this happen to the royal family? These were the people God chose to rule the nation. So where is God now? God *did* have something to say about this situation. In the law given to the Israelites, proper relationships between people were defined. Even though that culture allowed things like debt slavery or unequal treatment of women--things that we should not endorse--the law did a commendable job of defining and prohibiting a lot of unhealthy, destructive practices. The type of abuse committed by Amnon was not condoned. So one answer to the question, "Where is God in all of this?" is that God had already spoken, but those words of divine wisdom were ignored. If everyone were living according to the example and direction of God, especially the instruction given through Christ, then these problems would be greatly reduced, if not eliminated. But, as the old saying goes, "If toad frogs had wings they wouldn't bump their tails when they jumped."

It is of little use to know what God says about faithful living if a person is not going to at least attempt to live faithfully. The fact that God said certain types of abuse were wrong and sinful is of little consolation to victims like Tamar.

God's laws, or shall we say Christian values, are of little benefit if their powers of persuasion are not great enough to prevent individuals from transgressing them. Without owning or living by those values, they become little more than a standard of truth that amplifies the errors and sins of a society instead of a positive force that shapes healthy, respectful, faithful behavior. One of the greatest tasks for the Church is to cultivate a generation of believers and their families who actually attempt to practice the faith they affirm in theory within the arena of daily living.

Another thing the Scripture offers us when promises have been broken and values ignored is the assurance of God's constant, sustaining presence. We would like for it to be a protective and preventive presence, but that does not always happen. What we *are* promised is a loving, sustaining presence. The 23rd Psalm provides one of the most beautiful examples. "Even though I walk through the valley of the dark shadows,[33] I will fear no evil for you are with me . . . Your rod and your staff, they comfort me. You prepare a table before me in the presence of my enemies. You anoint my head with oil; my cup overflows . . . ." These songs of the heart speak about God's presence and dependability in times when we need a hand to help us through the darkness, when we need courage to face our enemies, and when we need a rod to guide or oil to sooth because our hurt is so great.

Someone once remarked to a friend, "Sometimes I would like to ask God why he allows violence, abuse and injustice when he could do something about it."

The friend replied, "Well why don't you ask God?"

The first friend answered, "Because I'm afraid God might ask me the same question."

That *is* a good question. If the values have been given and a better way is known, can we sit idly by with a clear conscience? The most useless character in the Tamar story was the king himself. Verse 21 says "when King David heard of all these things, he became very angry, but he would not punish his son Amnon because he loved him, for he was his first born." How many stories have we heard of people--mothers, fathers, siblings--who look the other way or refuse to intervene in abusive situations because of fears regarding reputation or misdirected anger? People with the power and authority to institute change, but who fail to do so because of preferential relationships, are nearly as disappointing as the promise breakers themselves.

When it comes to the family fault created by abuse and neglect, if nothing else, we can start with ourselves by listening and living up to the values God has given us. Then we will find strength to reach out, comfort others and help them do the same.

If you are a Promise Breaker currently abusing or neglecting a family member, or anyone else for that matter, **STOP!** All parts of your life, including that one, must be brought into conversation with the Spirit of God. The Power of the Gospel enables us to keep promises and respect the dignity of others. If you want to stop but cannot, ask for help.

If abuse and neglect are part of your current existence, don't suffer in silence. If the gospel really has the power to heal and transform, and if the Christian faith community really seeks to embody the teachings of Scripture, someone in your congregation or circle of friends should be able to serve as a confidant, a companion, a living presence to you. Don't underestimate the healing power of releasing the frustration and pain of your situation to a good, trustworthy listener. Often, it is the necessary beginning to emotional purging and cleansing the wounds you bear.

Finally, know from Scriptures like Psalm 23 that no valley is too deep or dark for God to enter. You never, ever suffer alone, except by choice!

FOR DISCUSSION

1. Which promises that you have made do you consider most important to the well-being of your family?

2. What promises made to you by members of your family would be most bothersome if broken?

3. How well does your family follow through on its commitments to one another? How can you improve in this area?

4. Can you identify any forms of abuse or neglect, whether verbal, physical or emotional, that are present in your current family relationship? How can they be addressed?

5. In what ways has God sustained you in situations of abuse and neglect?

Chapter 9

FAMILY BLESSINGS
Genesis 48

The sun sinks gracefully below the horizon as the family gathers at home after yet another long, busy day. Husband and wife have both put in eight hours on the job, ten counting travel time and errands. When their residence finally comes into sight, neither party is nearly as vibrant and perky as at the beginning of the day. They meet at home, where there is a brief reunion, maybe a kiss, perhaps just a grunt, along with a mechanical exchange of how their respective days were. As they share kitchen duties and prepare dinner, the children occupy themselves.

The children have also had a full day. There was school, plus an afternoon filled with extracurricular activities. The day's events eventually led to a day care center, where they remained until a parent picked them up on the trip home. Despite all these activities, *they are* as energetic as they were at eight a.m. There is a wrestling match over the computer mouse, and later over the TV remote control. The conflict quickly passes and soon they chase each other around the house, laughing, teasing, screaming as they enjoy themselves. The parents scold them once or twice, but the children know from the tone of their voices that they need not fear just yet, and so the chaos continues. Mother and father are happy to be reunited with the flesh of their flesh and bone of their bone after several hours apart; but an endless supply of energy continues to propel those little dynamo bodies belonging to the children. In a matter of minutes the one, last, good nerve the parents shared upon arrival at what should be their haven of peace is just about frazzled.

As the parents scurry around the kitchen cooking this and tossing that, the phone rings. It is a phone solicitor telling what great customers they are and offering five magazines with tantalizing titles like "Guns and Ammo" or, "Midwestern Mud Wrestlers" along with "Peacemakers Anonymous and other Well Known Martyrs." They are absolutely free, for only the price of the shipping and handling. In this case, "free" amounts to approximately twelve dollars a month. As the interrupted, irritated phone call recipient says "no" for the eighth time and hangs up the phone, the meat loaf starts to smell. The table is set and just as the parents are about to call the rest of the family to dinner, the phone rings again. It is yet another solicitor selling energy-saving light bulbs. All proceeds go to support the "Fraternal Order of Pestering Telemarketers."

Finally everyone is corralled into the dining room, where the middle child is in tears because they never did stop their rough-housing when you told them to the first five times. After putting an end to their making faces, kicking under the table, and blowing bubbles in their milk, a moment of peace settles around the table. It is perhaps the first time you have all been together in the same room all day. You are hungry, ready to devour anything that comes your way in a serving dish, as lunch seems eons ago. But before passing the first tray, there is a Pavlovian pause while someone blesses the food. There may even be a brief debate over whose turn it is to pray. Some nice words are uttered in God's direction, perhaps a memorized prayer. The final "amen" slips out of the mouth signifying to all it is safe to eat. The blessing is over and the normal noisy fare resumes. Preparing to eat can be a hectic experience.

For those who do not relate to this scenario, consider yourself fortunate. You probably live a slower, more relaxed pace of life. For those who do relate, take comfort that you are not alone. The above scenario is offered as a way to begin thinking about the role "blessing" plays in the family. The issue is not whether you pray before meals. The description is offered as an image that is a fairly accurate symbol of many family lives. Most of us are involved in a plethora of activities. They keep us busy. They excite us. They add meaning and a sense of purpose to our existence. Occasionally, they infuriate us. Most of all, they can leave us so frazzled that, if we aren't careful, we are at our absolute worst when we are with family. The irony--and possible absurdity--that we are at our worst with those we love the most should not be lost on us. Even so there are little places in our lives, tiny moments where we settle into peace, where we are united in harmony, where positive blessing occurs. Some of them are as absent-minded and on the outside apparently empty, even ritualistic or mechanical as some blessings at meal time. Yet their value is greater than we might suspect.

Previous chapters of this book have illustrated that several Bible stories offer words of wisdom on the type of destructive faults that often exist within families. They have illuminated the negative effects such faults will have if the work of God in our lives does not touch upon them. By identifying them, it is hoped the stories have helped name some of the things with which you have had to deal, or with which you need to deal, within your own family. Once identified I hope you find, with the assistance of the Holy Spirit, some power to address them.

Scripture also gives us a snapshot of a positive, healthy family moment. Such is the case in a story located in Genesis 48. The tale comes from the family of Jacob, a family whose life together was frequently interrupted by some of the very faults we have examined together. The scene occurs after the family's reunion with Joseph in Egypt, where he was a powerful figure in the Pharaoh's court. The passage is part of a deathbed blessing, which was a standard rite of passage among ancient Israelite families. This blessing contains positive family traits that can be instructional for us.

First, is the very mind set that *blessing* a family is part of our responsibility and part of what it means *to be* family. As a verb, the word "blessing" does double duty. Most importantly, it means to evoke and assist divine care within the family. Blessing was part of God's work in creation. It was a primary force in the covenant with the chosen family of Abram and Sara. In addition to that divine element, in a general sense, blessing also refers to the human effort to help bring happiness to the family. As illustrated in the covenant with Abram and Sara, even as they received God's blessing, they were to *be* a blessing to others.[34]

Admittedly, *blessing* may not make the short list of activities we regard as important within families. Sadly for some, families are simply people thrown together by passion or biological process who now have to endure each other's company. Such may be the case for a man or woman who makes an unwise selection of a mate and chooses to live in misery rather than take the all too common route of divorce. Another imaginable scenario of the "thrown together family" is the case of in-laws who have joined the family through various marriage covenants. For one reason or another, either or both parties would have preferred to have never met, let alone pretend to be family. A third example might involve siblings who are so different from one another, and whose relationships are so full of friction, or perhaps apathy, one can hardly believe they share the same gene pool. Other than biological ties or marriage connections, some families share little common ground. In these situations, the idea of *blessing* as part of family dynamics seems far removed.

Blessing is also difficult in situations where we think only in terms of what family could or should do *for* us. A husband who expects his wife to serve submissively as though she has no thoughts, no ideas, no dreams of her own is unlikely to consider his responsibility to inject a blessing into that relationship. A wife whose expectations of her husband lead her to continuously berate him for failing to provide for her as her father did will seldom consider the possibility that a positive contribution is needed from her. Children who, as adults, still believe their parents' first priority is to provide for them financially and always keep their room available for them, have not yet learned they are not the sole focus of the family. In these homes, *blessing* will be little more than imaginative fantasy.

Even in the best of situations and the happiest of families, blessing may be difficult at the end of a long day. It is not that we do not love our families, for we most certainly do. Irresponsibility is not the issue, for we are aware of our obligations. It is more a matter of the spirit being willing, but the flesh being weak. The demands of the work day and the pressures of life drain us, leaving us little to offer when we walk through the door of our homes. Two hours of playing on the living room floor with the children would be wonderful. A romantic evening with husband or wife would be rewarding. But despite good intentions, we cannot quite muster the energy to carry through on these nice ideas. In such instances, *blessing* and *family* are as naturally compatible as snow sledding in the tropics. What we discover is that before we can bless our families, we need time to ourselves to regroup and recuperate from the demands of the day.

With these, and many other possibilities, we may reach a place where the word *family* reminds us only of responsibility and headaches. Any of those scenarios can drive the concept of blessing further and further away until our family interaction is like an incident described by Joyce Landorf in her book *Irregular People*.

She tells of a woman in her thirties who learned that she needed a mastectomy. She and her mother seldom communicated, so the daughter was apprehensive about telling her mother of the upcoming surgery.

One day over lunch, she decided to reveal the news. "Mother, I just learned I am going to have a mastectomy."

The mother was silent.

The daughter asked if she had heard. The mother nodded her head. Then she calmly dismissed the subject by saying, "You know, your sister has the best recipe for chicken enchiladas."

That was nowhere near the response this daughter sought from her mother. The truth is that sometimes the individuals whom we most want to "be there" for us are not "there" when we need them. That is at least partially because the idea of family as a place of blessing which promotes divine care and contributes a compassionate response to even our worst news, is missing in many contemporary understandings of family. This tendency is reversed when families understand that blessing is part of what families do for each other.

Second, in the Genesis story we are told that Joseph brought his sons close to their grandfather Jacob, and that Jacob kissed and embraced them. The story models positive, loving touch. It accepts embrace and kiss as appropriate behavior between family members. One critique that is often levied against families, and against men and fathers in particular, is that there is not enough actual, physical contact within families. Touch is a powerful conveyor of love and affection.

A joke is told about a woman who was always

suffering from depression. She was continuously upset and unhappy. Her concerned husband took her to a psychiatrist.

The doctor listened to the couple talk about their relationship, and then said, "I have identified the problem and the treatment I prescribe is really quite simple." With that he went over to the man's wife, gathered her up in his arms and gave her a big kiss. He then stepped back and looked at the woman's glowing face and broad smile. Turning to the woman's husband, he said, "See! That's all she needs to put new life back into her."

Expressionless, the husband said, "Okay, doc. I can bring her in on Tuesdays and Thursdays, if that fits your schedule."

Curing depression is usually not that easy. Even so, the benefit and blessing that come from a caring touch is frequently underestimated. The tragedy is that just as progress was being made in that area, the issues of incest and sexual abuse injected an element of fear into many who recognize the problem of no contact but do not want to be falsely accused of having deviant motives. Even so, this family snapshot from Scripture reminds us that appropriate touch and embrace have a place in healthy families. It is up to us to discover how we can make that a part of our relationship.

Third, Jacob's act of blessing was filled with kind words, genuine wishes for the children's success, and a passing on of the faith tradition. As those two children sat on his lap enjoying their grandfather's embrace, they also heard and understood how glad their grandfather was to be with them. What is more important, they learned that the God of their grandparents and parents was also a God who would love and bless them.

In the midst of this blessing activity, Jacob crossed his hands and, in effect, gave the firstborn blessing, which was the most powerful family blessing a son could receive, to the younger of the two boys. While this switch troubled Joseph, there is something liberating in Jacob's actions. For in this transfer of blessing, it is possible that Jacob saw and acknowledged the real potential as well as real limitations of each of the children.

We may do our family members a disservice by telling them they can be whatever they want to be. The intent is to encourage the person, and that is an honorable goal. Yet everyone has limited abilities. When goals significantly outrace abilities, we discover that although we *can* be and do many things well, we may not be able to do *anything* we want to do well. It is one thing to encourage a child to pursue his or her dreams. It is another to burden that young life with unrealistic expectations. For instance, I appreciate the fact that my mother always believed in my abilities, yet did not insist on how they should be used.

Like a wise sage, Jacob encouraged the two boys to be what God called them to be rather than what birth order or family tradition expected of them. We should pray for such honest critiques and encouragement from those we call family.

Finally, the story contains one last noteworthy feature, namely, that Joseph bowed before his father. For most of us, this is an unheard of gesture in Western society, but for the Israelite culture of that period, it was a sign of honor and respect. In the context of this story, Joseph's bowing suggests that when we live in a family that understands and practices blessing its members, honor and respect are not so difficult.

What a positive family environment! It included the attitude of blessing, the elements of touch and embrace, plus kind words, all in the context of living and sharing the faith. These are all simple things. They cost nothing except time and effort. But their effects are as transformational and essential as yeast in bread.

The story gives us an ideal model. That is the goal. The world in which we try to appropriate this model requires that we add a dose of realism to this idealistic model. Not many of us will be like the television families of the Ozzie and Harriet Nelson household, or the Walton family, or the Cosby gang, where never is heard a discouraging word and no problem takes more than thirty minutes to resolve. If we are fortunate, we are not like the Dan and Roseanne Connor or the Al and Peg Bundy families either. But in today's society, there is a greater probability of fitting the latter model than the former one. If it is any consolation, even Jesus' family was one filled with faults. His closest kin ridiculed him for his claims to be a Messiah, at least for a while. But even if you do feel more like the Connors than the Waltons, learn to practice those elements of family blessing because, no matter how minuscule and rare, they can have an effect.

A story is told about a young man named Al who was a skilled artist, a potter. He had a wife and two fine sons. One night, his oldest son developed a severe stomachache. Thinking it was only some common intestinal disorder, neither Al nor his wife took the condition very seriously. But the malady was actually acute appendicitis, and the boy died suddenly that night.

Knowing the death could have been prevented if he had only realized the seriousness of the situation, Al's emotional health deteriorated under the enormous burden of his guilt. To make matters worse, his wife left him a short time later, leaving him alone with his six-year-old younger son. The hurt and pain of the two situations were more than Al could handle, and he turned to alcohol to help him cope. In time, Al became an alcoholic.

As the alcoholism progressed, Al began to lose everything he possessed. He lost his home, his land, his art objects, everything. Eventually, he died alone in a San Francisco motel room. When a friend heard of Al's death, he reacted with the same disdain the world shows for one who ends his life with nothing material to show for it. "What a complete failure! What a totally wasted life!"

As time went by, he was forced to reevaluate that harsh judgment. You see, he knew Al's other son, Ernie. Ernie was one of the kindest, most caring, most loving men he had ever known. He watched Ernie with his children and saw the free flow of love between them. He knew that kindness and caring had to come from somewhere.

He had never heard Ernie talk much about his father. One day he worked up his courage to ask him. He said, "I'm really puzzled by something. I know your father was basically the only one to raise you. What on earth did he do that you became such a special person?"

Ernie sat quietly and reflected for a few moments. Then he said, "From my earliest memories as a child until I left home at eighteen, Al came into my room every night, gave me a kiss and said, 'I love you, son.'" Tears came to the friend's eyes as he realized what a fool he had been to judge Al as a failure. [35]

Despite all the chaos and faults in Al's family, there were moments of blessing. Though they were not as numerous as we might hope, they were sufficient to stabilize those family faults in the next generation.

None of our families will ever be fault-free. Between outside pressures, personal issues, and the friction that comes simply by living under the same roof together where we share everything from toothpaste to living space, there will be moments when the faults shift and the foundations in our families shake. But there is reason for hope and optimism, for in the Scripture God has also provided us a practical model for healthy families. It can work for us all if we learn that the family blessing involves more than a brief prayer at mealtime.

FOR DISCUSSION

1. Does your family's current schedule provide adequate time together? If not, how can you change that situation?

2. Does your family convey blessing to all its members or not? Why do you answer as you do?

3. Who especially blesses you, and how do they do it? Make sure that person(s) knows how significant those things are to you.

4. What are some ways that you can become a greater source of God's blessing for your family?

Conclusion

FAMILY TIES
Romans 8:1-17

There is no denying the fact that I am getting older. Of course I have been for more than three decades, but it is becoming more obvious now. A grey hair here or an achy joint there catch my attention. I recently received a major reminder of this trend. My baby sister married a few months ago, as if her graduating from college were not enough of a reminder! The youngest chick has left the nest. Little Jeanne, or Dink, as we used to call her, is all grown up.

She was the little tag-along who wanted to do and who wanted to mimic everything her older siblings did. This is the sister whose day could hardly get any better if her older brother would let her ride in his car. This full-grown woman is the same person, who as a child, cried when her mamma told her she had to wear clothes when she went outside the house. Do not misunderstand. They were not really optional indoors either, but they were a little more essential outside.

Times have surely changed. This once-little-girl is now a college graduate with a job. She is making real money, and for the first time having to figure out what to do with it. I remember the day she went out and bought a new car all by herself, without seeking any advice from the rest of us. Though I really wanted to advise her to wait a few months and accumulate a nice savings before buying, I kept my mouth shut. It is hard to argue convincingly when I did the same thing as a high school graduate.

As an older brother, I am happy that Jeanne is doing well and her life has direction. Not long after college graduation, she confided to me that she felt like those years studying radiology were finally producing dividends. I told her I was sure she now knew a lot about radiology, but thought that during those years in college, she had also been studying Jeanne-ology. Some people just do not appreciate a good play on words. She looked at me like I was a cracked nut, which reminded me that not everything about our relationship has changed with age. I replied this Jeanne-ology was spelled with a J not a G. I meant she had engaged, not in a study of family ancestry, but in a study of Jeanne. During those collegiate years, she had studied herself, though perhaps without knowing it. She had learned a bit of who she was, what her goals and dreams were, and knew a little better of how she fit into our family, and that she really did belong there.

Many years ago, Dee, the sister immediately ahead of Jeanne, came home from high school one day terribly frustrated. She said, "I'm sick and tired of being a little sister."

Even a smart alec older brother knew better than to retort, “That’s okay, I’m tired of having a little sister. Let’s solve this problem!” With a touch of infuriation she went on to explain, “Everybody at school remembers you as the smart one and Kelly as the athlete. I just want to know who am I supposed to be? What is my place in this family?” That was a fair question for her, and for us all!

Fortunately, she found her place. If it were that difficult for the third sibling, the fourth probably didn’t find it any easier. Seeing my little sister grown up, graduated, and now married, sandwiched around the death of my father and my maternal grandmother, unleashed that reflective portion of my brain to consider family ties. What do they really mean? How do they change over the years?

If there is one thing I am certain of on this subject, it is that all our roles have changed with time. And whether or not you’ve realized it, that has happened to your family ties as well. It happens to us all because as time marches on, it insists we follow along. Those who try to deny the changes usually succeed only in making life miserable for everyone involved, whether that is the parent who cannot accept that a child is maturing, or children who cannot fathom that their parents are aging, or some other changing tie.

Our family roles change with time. I watched my father go from farmer to minister to an early grave. I have observed my mother mature from nurturing housewife into a certified public accountant. My sisters and I have gone from diapers to diplomas to the pursuit of our dreams.

The gaps between the momentous occasions were filled with laughter and tears, happiness and anger, good and bad, and occasional boredom. Sometimes we were laughing with each other and sometimes at each other. Sometimes we were angry for each other, and sometimes we were infuriated with each other. All of those things--every one of them, bar none--are part of our family ties.

Birth, blood, adoption or marriage may have originally initiated the family connection, but it is the common experience together that maintains the group's connectedness. Even at age thirty-eight, I realize my family is not finished. My role will continue to change. I went from teasing older brother to the example of how to lead your parents through your own adolescence and drive them nuts as you do it, to an adult whose advice may be worth considering. Now I find myself being friend, cheerleader and occasional adviser to them all. Who knows what future changes will bring?

Through all the changing roles and in the midst of strained, strengthened, or reshaped ties, it has become obvious that the most important feature is that the family tie remained constant. They were always there for me, either in person or in spirit. When I was in a bus wreck, my father was there, holding me in his arms while they rushed me to the hospital. When I tried to grow up faster than I should, my mother and father were there to deter me. When I delivered my retiring address to a couple of thousand people as the North Carolina Future Farmers of America State President, they led the standing ovation. When I preached my first sermon, they were in the congregation supporting me. The tie was always there, and I was always connected. Even if I were especially irritating on some days, which I certainly was on occasion, the tie was never severed.

I have never doubted that I was a Marshall. That is one of the benefits of being the first child. There are no older siblings around who get their kicks trying to convince you that you don't really belong! Being a Marshall is not necessarily any better or worse than being a member of any other family. What is important is that being a Marshall meant I belonged to a particular group. That in itself is important because none of us needs to float or drift around disconnected for very long. In addition to that, the family to whom we are tied, is a group that influences how we think, feel, and behave. That may produce positive, constructive traits, or negative, destructive tendencies, depending on the health of the family that influenced us. But in either case, our family ties will affect us.

When I was a teenager, a family at the Friends Meeting I attended adopted a young child named Ike from a foster program. I admire people who share themselves in this way because this is seldom an easy task. This child had some personal challenges and had been bounced around from home to home. This family made a commitment to offer him a more stable family tie. Like any family, I suspect they experienced some trying moments over the years, but as far as I know, they handled them all with grace and dignity.

The first Sunday they brought the child to church, proudly introducing him as *their son*, was especially memorable. The congregation welcomed him and called him by name: "Hi, Ike. We're glad you're here." He quickly announced to us that he had a new family now, and so he wanted to be called by a new name. He would like to be called by his middle name, Steven.

Not belonging had affected him. Being initially welcomed and then quickly rejected in various foster situations, had left him fragile, insecure, untied from the family, so to speak. But this situation felt different. A new family tie had already initiated a new way for him to understand himself.

The effect of the family tie is nothing short of incredible. It can be life-changing, even transforming, to the point of taking on a new name. I share these reflections as a means of encouraging you to reminisce about your own particular family ties. How have they shaped you? In what ways have they helped you? Supported you? Perhaps even disappointed you? Most importantly, have you considered how the concept of a family tie relates to your relationship with God?

"Family ties" is an appropriate image for understanding Paul's words from Romans 8. The apostle gets a bit involved in his discussion of law and the Spirit, of sin and overcoming sin, and of what controls our mind. But the primary point is his insistence that there is now no condemnation for those who have been awakened by the mysterious work of Christ in our hearts. There is now no rejection. There is no cause for insecurity. Those who are in Christ Jesus are to recognize that they are part of God's family.

To fully appreciate the weight of this statement, we need to remember Paul's discussion at the end of chapter 7. There, Paul's words reveal he is in absolute inner turmoil. One can easily imagine his stomach in knots. He struggles because he knows what God wants from him. He understands what he wants to do as a Christian. But so often he discovers that he is powerless to be the person he wants to be. He says, "I can will what is right, but I cannot do it. For I do not do the good

I want, but the evil I do not want is what I do."[36] Having recognized that struggle within himself, and as a good Jew knowing that under the law this dilemma is not good news for those who wish to be faithful to God, Paul makes the remarkable statement which opens chapter 8: "There is now no condemnation for those who are in Christ Jesus." Why? Because when Christ entered his, and our, lives, a family tie was formed. All who are led by the Spirit of God are children of God. We can approach God as Abba, as Father, as a loving parent. As family members, we are joint heirs with Christ. We share a special relationship to God. All in the family will receive an inheritance from their Heavenly Father.

If you consider yourself to be in Christ, if you believe Christ's death and resurrection has set you free, if you know that the Spirit of life is yours, then you have the most important family tie of all. You have a place among God's children. You belong. That is a message which, even if heard, sometimes never ties into our self-understanding. Perhaps it is because our own personal family experience has been negative, and consequently, the thought that we are part of God's family stirs absolutely nothing within us. Possibly it is because in our understanding of God, disciplining, judgmental, even vengeful characteristics dominate our expectations. That perception may be related to our reading of Scripture or the type of care we received from our earthly parents. It could be that we aren't certain of who we are or how we fit into the family of faith. We have not done our own "Jeanne-ology" so to speak, and are therefore unclear of what family ties bind us to God. Perhaps we wonder whether or not we *really* belong. But we need to know, because understanding that we are loved and that we belong has a powerful effect on who we are and what we become.

Mary Ann Bird wrote a moving story about belonging, entitled "The Whisper Test." It is a true story from her own life. She writes: "I grew up knowing I was different, and I hated it. I was born with a cleft palate, and when I started school, my classmates made it clear to me how I must look to others: a little girl with a misshapen lip, crooked nose, lopsided teeth and garbled speech."

"When schoolmates would ask, 'What happened to your lip?' I'd tell them I'd fallen and cut it on a piece of glass. Somehow it seemed more acceptable to have suffered an accident than to have been born different. I was convinced that no one outside my family could love me."

"There was, however, a teacher in the second grade that we all adored--Mrs. Leonard by name. She was short, round, happy--a sparkling lady. Annually, we would have a hearing test. I was virtually deaf in one of my ears; but when I had taken the test in past years, I discovered that if I did not press my hand as tightly upon my ears as I was instructed to do, I could pass the test."

"Mrs. Leonard gave the test to everyone in the class, and finally it was my turn. I knew from past years that as we stood against the door and covered one ear, the teacher sitting at the desk would whisper something and we would have to repeat it back . . . things like, 'The sky is blue' or 'Do you have new shoes?' I waited there for those words, which God must have put into her mouth, those seven words which changed my life. Mrs. Leonard said in her whisper, 'I wish you were my little girl.'"[37]

With that one simple sentence, an incredible tie was formed. Not all family ties are biological ones. Family ties are found where we are loved. They abound where we are wanted. Family is where we belong. Family ties are especially found wherever God is. God says to each one of us, "I wish you were my little girl, or my little boy. My daughter. My son." Paul teaches us that God went one step further than simply wishing it. God made it a reality through the work of Christ, in one sense adopting us, and in another sense simply reminding us of the divine intention at creation and reclaiming us.

Are you aware of your family ties? You need to understand that you are tied into God's family. Even if your earthly family has not measured up to normal expectations and you feel uncared for, you are wanted in God's family. You need never feel you do not belong. You need only delight in the Spirit of Christ. Rejoice in the Spirit of Life and let it set you free. Like any family, your role will change as you mature in the faith. Sometimes those changes are challenging. Like any family, as we live and love together, there will be laughter and tears, happiness and anger, some good and some bad. But if you are in Christ Jesus, you will never, ever, face condemnation. Do your own version of "Jeanne-ology" and you will discover it for yourself. If you are in Christ Jesus, you are family. You belong. Period.

FOR DISCUSSION

1. How well do you fit into your family? Do you sense you belong, and your place is secure? Or do you feel left out, and unattached?

2. Do you understand your place in God's family?

3. How does understanding that you are a child of God change your self-perspective?

4. How can understanding that you are a child of God help heal any faults in your family?

NOTES

1 Genesis 1:27.

2 Genesis 2:18-25.

3 Genesis 12:1-4

4 Deuteronomy 24:17-22; 25:5-10.

5 Matthew 10:34-39; Luke 14:26.

6 Mark 10:2-12.

7 Ephesians 5:22-33.

8 Ephesians 6:1-4.

9 F. Buechner, *Whistling in the Dark*, (San Francisco: Harper & Row, 1988), p. 47.

10 G. Recker, *Counseling Families*, (Dallas: Word, 1988), p. 12.

11 J. Craig and L. Elmiger, *Family: Drawing the Circle Wide*. (New York: General Global Ministries, 1994), p. 9.

12 *Grace in Word and Action*, July 1996, p. 3.

13 Jeremiah 29:13.

14 Luke 15.

15 I John 4:8; James 3:13-18

16 *Pastor's Story File*, March 1985, p. 3-4.

17 *Ibid.*

18 II Timothy 3:5.

19 *Utne Reader*, May/June 1994, p. 66.

20 *Ibid.*

21 Genesis 28:10-22.

22 Genesis 30:25-43.

23 J. Canfield and M. Hansen, *Chicken Soup for the Soul*, (Deerfield Beach: Health Communications, 1993) pp. 69-71.

24 R. Fulghum, *It Was On Fire When I Lay On It*, (New York: Ivy Books, 1988), pp. 25-29.

25 *Parables, Etc.*, August 1981.

26 J. Larsen, "A Story For Valentine's Day," as found in *Chicken Soup for the Soul*, pp. 43-45.

27 Adapted from T. Dobson, *Safe and Alive*, (Los Angeles: JP Tarcher, 1981), pp. 128-132.

28 Genesis 29:17.

29 Ecclesiastes 1:2.

30 Noah Ben Shea, *Jacob the Baker*, (New York: Villard Books, 1989), pp. 27-28.

31 I Samuel 12:10.

32 J.Scieszka & L. Smith, *The Stinky Cheese Man and other Fairly Stupid Tales*, (New York: Viking, 1992).

33 "Dark shadows" is a better translation of the Hebrew than the traditional "shadow of death."

34 Genesis 12:1-4.

35 B. Gee, "A Legacy of Love," as found in *Chicken Soup for the Soul*, pp. 117-18.

36 Romans 7:18-19.

37 *Homiletics*, April-June 1994, p. 25.